MW01289979

From Struggle to Victory

Victory

My journey of overcoming mental illness, Conversion Disorder, PNES, and self-harm

OLIVIA LODI

From Struggle To Victory

Copyright © 2018 Olivia Lodi

All rights reserved.

ISBN: 9781720063117

Cover design by Rebeca from Fiverr.com

Images from:

Dropbox.com

Callie Sullivan

Used by Permission.

Formatted by Olivia Lodi

This book is dedicated to all the people across the globe

who struggle daily with mental health issues,

and each day come through it stronger

than before.

TABLE OF CONTENTS

Forward

By Charis Leigh Henson

When Olivia Lodi told me she was writing this book, I was thrilled. I knew she and this book were special. I'd been waiting for a book on mental health to be written by a Christian who wasn't afraid to be human. For far too long mental health has been shut up in closets and silenced by the world, and I regret to say by the church as well. The Church could use a good waking up in this area so that we can help our brothers and sisters who struggle. How are we to help without being better equipped?

Her insights as a survivor will have you thinking deeply about how you treat the mentally and physically ill, and her stark honesty will make you weep with repentance.

But before you proceed to her story, a word of caution: Olivia has chosen to be as frank as possible about all that she has experienced. If you are struggling with any of the illnesses discussed in this book, reader discretion is advised. Olivia is not being graphic for the sake of being graphic, but the subject matter is still weighty, heavy, and difficult to talk about let alone to read in solitude. So please, take care of yourself. If you find yourself needing to stop, please do so. Also know that you are not alone.

And now it is with great pleasure that Olivia invites you into her story to learn and to heal.

Preface

Hi! My name is Olivia Lodi, and by the time this book is published I'll be twenty-three years old. I was born into a Christian home and am the eldest of six children, with one sister and four brothers. Originally from California, my family and I moved twice before finding a home in the city just outside of Dallas, Texas. We lived there for ten years prior to making a final move to the country, where we now reside with a few acres and some farm animals.

I have dealt with chronic health issues for most of my life. When I was almost four years old I began having grand mal seizures, resulting in the diagnosis of Epilepsy. I eventually did grow out of them right before my teenage years, but other problems began arising soon afterwards. I was in and out of doctors' offices and hospitals, trying to figure out what was going on and not getting a whole lot of answers. Migraines, trouble breathing, heart irregularities, food allergies, and stomach problems are just to name a few.

During that time, our family was missionaries in Texas for twelve years, raising our own support, working in the state-side office, and pouring our finances, time, and life into ministry. After twelve years, we found out the truth: that the place we were working at was actually a cult. The aftermath left a large amount of mental and emotional damage. I also experienced many deaths, including children, and saw and dealt with a few deceased people while working as a firefighter which would later come back as traumatizing memories.

Because of all these things that happened in my life, I became depressed, and easily anxious. I tried suicide as a way of escape twice, and failed. The thoughts in my mind tortured me daily. Over time and effort, I found ways to cope with the mental illnesses that I had. The journey has been long and hard, but I feel like now is my time to share my testimony with you, and show those who struggle that they are not alone.

So now it begins. Here is my story.

PART 1: ANXIETY

CHAPTER 1

Breathe

One gorgeous afternoon in October 2010, my family -- mom, dad, and four siblings -- was at a housewarming party for some friends. I'd had an emotionally rough week leading up to that Saturday, with a large amount of anger, loneliness and depression affecting my everyday life, but was at that time finally feeling happy and free. The air was perfect, and I was running around our friends' backyard chasing some of the kids while the adults stayed inside and talked. Life was good...for once. The light was beginning to fade in the clear Texas sky as the sun was setting for the night.

Suddenly, one of the parents came out of the house with a grave face. He asked us all to pray for his wife who had just passed out inside their home and told us to stay outside for a while until they could figure out what to do, to avoid crowding a pregnant sick mother. My heart sank into my stomach when I realized how serious the situation was. We did pray, but I decided to at least go see what was going on. I was only fifteen years old at the time, but already knew that I wanted to help people with their physical needs once I had graduated high school and was old enough to attend college, so my natural reaction was to see if I could help. I mean, I couldn't just stand around and wonder.

I walked over to the back door and let myself in. There were already eight adults standing around her, trying to take her blood pressure and talking amongst each other, discussing the next plan of action. This mom was laying on the ground, with her legs up on a chair to help get the blood to her head. The home blood pressure monitor was showing that her pressure was not good and was way too low. Her face was white and her breathing was shallow. She was five months pregnant with her fourth child, which put her at risk for certain conditions and caused a great amount of concern for the friends around her.

I stood there shocked. Things didn't look good. I quickly started becoming short of breath myself, and very panicky. My chest was tightening and my heart was racing. *Dang it.* All I wanted to do was help, and instead I was having this weird reaction to the situation. I had never felt this badly before. It felt as if my lungs were closing up fast, just standing there in the living room.

What was going on? Why couldn't I breathe?

Dizziness started setting in, and I realized that I needed fresh air. The family had decided to call an ambulance to help out the pregnant mom, and I just couldn't handle it anymore. By the time I got outside, I'd burst into tears and was gasping for air, shaking like I had the flu. My heart was racing so fast and I thought I was going to pass out, feeling like I was on my way out of this world. Just when things had finally gotten better for me emotionally, my body collapsed with some strange condition.

I found one of my own friends that was attending the party, and tried to quickly explain how I felt, with the small amount of air that I had left. He helped me to sit down and put my head in between my knees, but that didn't work. I still couldn't breathe, and felt like the whole world was crashing in on me. I was in the front yard when the firefighters and ambulance crew showed up. I didn't want to be noticed, because although I wasn't sure if I was going to live, I knew that it was more important for our friend to be taken care of, without me distracting them.

So I sat in a far corner of the yard watching, and trying to survive. They put her on the stretcher, and wheeled her into the ambulance to be transported to the hospital, where she was to be treated and released later that night.

I tried to calm down and breathe normally, but it took about thirty minutes for my body to regulate itself. During that time, it felt like someone was sitting on my chest, and trying to choke me. My lungs hurt, and I couldn't help but freak out. After feeling this way for so long, any air I could get was a blessing. I eventually was able to get control of my breathing, and though tired, was breathing a sigh of relief. At that point I realized that I wasn't going to die, and I wouldn't have to say my goodbyes, or worry about if I had lived a fruitful life.

But it sure had felt like a brush with death.

This was my first real serious encounter with chronic anxiety and panic attacks that I can remember, and something that is not easily forgotten. It was in fact the beginning of many years of anxiety suffering that was not well understood by most. At the time of this first major attack, I honestly didn't know what was going on. It was absolutely terrifying and I wasn't sure why I was having so much trouble all of a sudden breathing. The whole thing came on so fast, and I thought that maybe I was developing asthma or something related to that.

Every few weeks to a month, I would have another attack and eventually convinced my mom to take me to the doctor. I needed something to help relieve this feeling of death; this pain and terror of not being able to breathe.

It was a few months after that gorgeous evening in October that I had an appointment set up with my family doctor. I was having some trouble breathing the morning of the visit, and I was sure the doctor could help me. My mom and I walked into the room and waited to be seen. My chest was tightening, my lungs were closing up, and I was becoming really agitated because of the fact that I needed air. I sat on the examining table, leaning forward, trying to somehow open up my airway. The doctor was taking forever to come in. Did he not understand how bad it was? What was holding him up?

Finally after what seemed like ages of waiting, he came in and of course asked what was going on. I wanted to scream at him. Didn't he see what the problem was? I forced myself to push what little air I could out of my lungs as I tried to explain what had been happening over the last couple months. The doctor took out his stethoscope and listened to my lungs. He asked me to take a deep breath -- but that was almost impossible for me to do, considering how tight my chest was. He said that everything looked clear, but he was going to check one more thing. The doctor walked out, and came back two minutes later with a device to check my oxygen output, or otherwise known as peak expiratory flow. I was told to blow as hard as I could into this tube, and did that three times. Surely this thing would show what was wrong with my lungs! The doctor looked at me, smiled, and told me that there was nothing wrong with me physically. He said I was probably just stressed, and told me to calm down.

I could not believe my ears. *Nothing wrong?* Just look at me! You can't just tell me to "calm down." Heck no. I was more frustrated and mad than ever before. This doctor had thrown off my symptoms as just stress, and I was not about to accept that as fact. I was sitting there on his examining table, hardly able to get air in my lungs, and was visibly ticked off that this guy was pretending to not notice anything...essentially telling me it was my fault. I started becoming very dizzy, turned white, and whispered that I was passing out. He asked if I thought I could walk out of there so mom could take me home, and I quietly responded with a shocked "no." Mom helped me lay down where I was at, and the doctor left, saying to go by the front desk before we leave, and that I would be fine. After about ten minutes of lying there, I started to feel a little bit better, and was able to slowly walk out to the car. My head was spinning a thousand miles a minute with so many different emotions that I didn't know how to control.

I was angry. I was sad. I was ticked off, and frustrated. I was tired and confused. This professional that I had trusted just squashed any hope for receiving help that I had left.

About one year later, I was officially diagnosed with anxiety by a different doctor, and struggled deeply to come to terms with that diagnoses. Most people thought of it as my fault, because it was supposedly something I could "control." But that couldn't be farther from the truth. I needed someone who could understand what I was going through. Someone who could show me how to cope with this new mental illness.

CHAPTER 2

Calm in the Storm

Growing up as a teenager with chronic anxiety was a very difficult thing to deal with. Hardly anyone I knew could understand what I was going through and encourage me through it. So instead, it was something that was used against me, one that people would throw back in my face and frustrate me with. They would do that by blaming me, and shrugging my symptoms or problems off as nothing, like it was no big deal. I was to them, obviously "out of control." It wasn't until many years later, that I discovered the truths about anxiety, how to cope with it, and how to help others. These discoveries I would like to share with you, since there is a growing number of people being diagnosed each year with this mental issue, and I think more people need to understand what to do.

One of the biggest things about anxiety (as well as almost all mental illnesses), is that it is not something completely in your control, no matter what other people think. It is a disorder that makes your body react to certain situations, and it's a completely terrifying experience. Most of the people that I interacted with told me that my anxiety attacks -- otherwise known as panic attacks -- were my fault, and something I could have prevented. That only created more anxiety and frustration, because I knew that it wasn't true, but nobody was telling me any different which made it hard to believe anything else.

When having a panic attack, it can hit you out of nowhere and for no particular reason that you can think of. Sometimes there is an obvious trigger, like a place or person that has a traumatic memory attached, or being around too many people, or driving on a freeway or road where you had previously had an accident a few months or years prior. But not every attack has an obvious or understandable reason behind it. I personally didn't know where most of my own panic attacks came from.

Once your body gets into its attacking mode, your heart rate will increase dramatically, your chest will tighten where it feels like someone is squeezing you to death, you will be shaky, you won't be able to breathe, you may become nauseous or even vomit, your hands and feet might get numb and tingly, and it seems like you are literally *drowning* with no one to save you.[1] It is also closely linked with depression.[2]

Sounds rough, right? It feels like death. There can be a tremendous fear that develops as you drown on the floor. The problem is, people don't know how to help. One huge thing I want to stress, is **do not** tell the anxiety sufferer to "calm down." This is the most worn-out phrase that I know, and is the worst one I've heard. This person *cannot control* what is going on in their body. If they could have just simply calmed down, they would have. Seriously, who would purposefully let this continue to torment them? No, telling them to calm down will make things even worse.

A few ways that you can help someone around you who is having an anxiety attack are as follows:

---

[1] "Anxiety Disorders." *National Institute of Mental Health*, 2016, nimh.nih.gov/health/topics/anxiety-disorders/index.shtml. Accessed 19 Aug 2018

[2] "The Link Between Depression and Other Mental Illnesses." *WebMD*, 2018, webmd.com/depression/guide/link-to-other-mental-illnesses#2. Accessed 19 Aug 2018

Be Gentle: Even though seeing a loved one in this situation can be scary, you have to be gentle and calm with them. You need to be strong *for* them; not controlling or losing your temper because they won't listen to you. Just being there for someone, being present, can be a comforting thing. They may need space because it feels like they're suffocating, so respect that request if that is what they need most.

Reassure: Make sure to reassure whoever is going through this attack, not that everything is okay, but that "we're going to get through this." When a friend or family member told me that everything was going to be okay, or that everything was fine, it actually made the attack worse because I became frustrated. During that time, I could not believe that everything was okay...because it wasn't. I didn't feel like people understood what was going on, which resulted in more frustration and an even harder time breathing. Even though saying that phrase is not a bad thing, it's just not the right one, at least it wasn't for me. The most reassuring thing that could be said is, "we will get through this together." Knowing that you have at least one person who won't leave and who's got your back is a comforting thought.

So be there and let them know.

Back Rub: Some people like to be touched. It can create a sense of safety and cause relaxation. Not everyone does, though, so make sure to ask if it's okay for you to gently rub their back. Don't do a back massage by any means, just a gentle back rub to show that you're there and that you care.

Breathe: One thing that may be helpful is to have the person breathe *with* you. Look each other in the eyes and breathe together to help slow down their already rapid breathing. It won't work right away, but over time their breathing will stabilize. You will need to tell them to keep going when they start to give up. Make sure you are not forceful though, but rather reassuring during this whole process. It is not at all easy to get your body to calm down and regulate after so much adrenaline that has put you in a fight or flight mode.

Encourage: Saying words of encouragement is always beneficial. Telling them that they've got this, that they are doing really well, that they can keep fighting -- all of those things will help quite a bit. Sometimes just reminding them how strong they are, how smart, how beautiful, how loved, or how awesome they are, can boost their confidence and put a spark of hope back into their life to replace the anxiety. Do not repeatedly say these things over and over, because it can become annoying quite quickly and create more anxiety. Rather, make sure to tell them at least one of these encouragements once or twice throughout the attack.

Ask: Something beneficial to helping a friend suffering with a panic attack would be to ask what would be best for them. Some people honestly need distance when going through an attack, so ask before you do anything. Communication is needed in almost all situations, including this one, so be sure to ask them if it's okay for you to talk with them, to rub their back, or hold their hand. You're welcome to ask if they need anything, but don't become annoyed if they don't know how to answer that question. Most times when I had a panic attack, I had no idea what I needed. I was just trying to survive. So please ask but be okay if they don't know.

Fill the Need: If you have a friend or loved one dealing with an anxiety attack, you will probably have a strong desire to help them in any way. They may not know what they need, so if you feel like there is something that might need to be done, go fill it and then let them know that it's there. An example might be that they look quite uncomfortable. You could bring out a pillow or a blanket, set it next to them, and tell them it's there if they need it. Another idea might be to fill a glass of water, since breathing fast can make their mouth very dry. Don't hand the water to them but put it close by and let them know it's there. That way you are still communicating, filling a potential need, not forcing anything, and giving them any space they might be requesting. If they do ask for help in a certain area, be there for them and be ready to fill the need.

For all of the people reading this book who deal with anxiety, please know that you are definitely not alone. In fact, anxiety is the "most common mental illness in the US, affecting 40 million adults in the United States". [3] It also affects 25.1% of children between 13-18 years old.

Don't ever think you're the only one. It is a frustrating issue for sure, and it can be extremely scary -- that is all normal. It's not an easy illness to tackle, but you *can* make progress. You *can* get better and learn how to manage your anxiety. There are things that you can do to help lessen the amount of panic attacks that you have. Here are a few that have been helpful for me in eliminating some of the stress that would cause an attack.

---

[3] "Facts and Statistics." *Anxiety and Depression Association of America*, 2010-2018, adaa.org/about-adaa/press-room/facts-statistics. Accessed 19 Aug 2018

Get rest: Make sure you get enough sleep at night, and don't overbook yourself. You need time by yourself each day to recover and rejuvenate your mind and body, whether in the evening before bed, in the morning after you wake up, or in the afternoon. Just make sure you get a chance to take care of *you*, while in the midst of a normal but busy life. Having too many things to do can also cause extra anxiety, so try to space things out and plan accordingly whenever possible. If you are having a busy season, make an appointment to rest a little bit throughout the week to help you get through that time. It is definitely okay to have plans, do things, and be busy for a period of time -- it's not a bad thing. I don't recommend not doing anything at all because you need motivations and friendships. Just be sure to take care of yourself as much as you can. Also know your limits; figure out what you can handle, and what you can't, and work around that making sure to get quality sleep in the process.

Enjoy Life: Hang out with a few friends during the week. Have fun, and make sure to throw in some laughter too, because laughter is good medicine! Go out and do a favorite hobby, just sit and talk with a friend, or go grab a cup of coffee with someone you enjoy hanging out with. Doing something fun can help dissolve the stress and anxiety you feel.

Exercise: Go out into the fresh air and take a walk around the neighborhood. You could go biking, jogging, swimming, or running. Being outdoors, especially when the sun is out, is very healthy. The environment and change of scenery from the indoors can breathe new life and energy into your body.

Talk: Make sure you are talking to someone about how you feel, whether to a friend, family member, or counselor. Getting things off your chest will help it not get all pent up inside, only to explode in a panic attack sometime later. It's okay to feel. It's okay to get it all out - - in fact, I highly recommend it. Talking helps with processing the situation, and how it makes you feel, giving you a relief of the burden you carry.

See a professional: The best thing you can do is go to someone who is trained to know how to treat this type of mental illness. They can help you find the best treatment for your anxiety, and listen to what you are suffering with. I know that seeing a counselor and a psychiatrist helped me learn how to manage my anxiety. There are different therapies that are meant to help lessen the anxiety you have, such as Cognitive Behavior Therapy (CBT) and Exposure Therapy. Those can be read about in detail on the website located here: nimh.nih.gov/health/topics/anxiety-disorders/index.shtml.

Medicine: Sometimes we try every option from our ideas at home, but it doesn't always work. Some people, like me, need more intensive treatment...or rather, additional treatment like medicine. Taking meds is not always a bad thing, and in this case can be a really good thing. Finding the right medication that will fit your need is a very relieving discovery to say the least. It can truly help your body not get into a panic mode as frequently, and it can help it regulate itself.

Prayer: If you are a religious person, praying can be a calming action. Having a God who is always available, One who will never leave you, One who listens to whatever you have to say, and is constant, can bring peace in the midst of chaos. To know someone who is with you no matter what, even when other people aren't, is an incredible thought. If you have no one else to talk to, talk to God. He wants to hear from you, and wants to know exactly how you feel...not just the good, but the bad and the ugly. It's okay to be frustrated, and to yell; it can end up being a very healing process. He understands. And just know that He's there for you!

Breathe: When in the midst of a panic attack, try to take deep controlled breaths as much as you can. Don't expect yourself to be able to take numerous deep breaths in a row, but try and do one or two per 30 seconds to one minute. Gradually increase when you can, and don't give up.

Arm Position: Put your arms above your head to open up your airway, and allow more needed oxygen to come in. Your lungs will be able to get more airflow, increase oxygen to your brain, and allow you to slow down your breathing. Many people suggest putting your head between your knees, but that does not work. So I would advise that you only try positioning your arms above your head and sitting up as straight as possible.

Doing these things can greatly help you in beating this illness of anxiety one day at a time. Just know that you *are* strong, and if you put your mind to it, you can overcome this controlling enemy. You can do it.

PART 2: POST TRAUMATIC STRESS DISORDER

CHAPTER 3

The Suffering of Sacrifice

In June of 2003, my parents and three siblings at the time packed up our three bedroom house in Lakewood, Colorado, and moved to Carrollton, Texas to be part of a missions organization. We were considered missionaries in the United States, and served at the headquarters to help with state-side inventory, finances, advertisement, fundraising, and administration. There were different departments within these types of categories to help run the ministry such as Information Technology department, Graphics department, Communications department, Volunteer department, Writing department, Missions department, Call Center, and many more. We raised most of the funds in the States and sent the money over to Asia to continue the ministry there. The goal was to raise up local missionaries within South Asia, help plant churches, start schools for kids, have a working hospital, and help provide work opportunities for the people in that area.

As I grew up a missionary kid, I quickly tried to make friends with the other children that were there. It was difficult though, since I didn't "fit in" with the girls my age that I wanted to be friends with, and I couldn't understand what was wrong with me. I had a few friends, though not many, but I considered everyone on staff there, family. We were all pretty close, since we only had each other, and weren't really allowed to get involved in the local community per leadership rules. They wanted everyone fully devoted to the ministry.

My family bounced around churches for a little while until we found one we all liked for the most part. I made a few more friends there, but we hardly ever got to hang out outside of church because of how far everyone lived. So, I did a lot of hanging out with my family and volunteering any time I had at the ministry.

My whole life revolved around ministry work, traveling with my family to support-raise, being different than everyone else in the world and trying to be okay with that, not living with much, and always knowing that thinking about myself was selfish. But there were multiple things I had to deal with during those years. I struggled with finding friends, and always gravitated toward the young adults since they were "fun" and a little more accepting of me. The friendships never lasted very long though, and my heart was consistently getting broken. I dealt with numerous health issues during this time that were not being resolved and felt like people kept looking down upon me and judging me because of them, rolling their eyes because I was such an inconvenience. As a result, I had to hide my issues, and pretend that everything was fine.

My mom had two miscarriages before she was able to have two more boys, and that hurt me to the core. Later, our family had to deal with a CPS (child protective services) incident since my littlest brother waddled off in the neighborhood when we had turned around for literally a few seconds. The police gave a good report, but CPS were knocking on our door the next day, and the questions they asked scarred me for life.

I'd had epilepsy as a child for eight years which I vividly remember, so when one of my young brothers had his first grand mal seizure, I became angry with myself because I had thought it was my fault. I later found out there was no way it could be my fault since that's not how epilepsy works, but my heart still throbbed, seeing such a young child turn blue with nothing I could do to help.

Life was hard.

I started going through emotional teenage stuff on top of everything else, and became a very angry person, though I kept a lot of it to myself or contained in my room. My mom and I would fight frequently and never come to an agreement. I almost ran away twice, because of how much hate I had in my heart. Working at the ministry became a burden, but I did it anyway. I kept a lot of things to myself, and stuffed it away internally. But on October 29th, 2010, God spoke to me, and I rededicated my life to Him. My life forever changed. I started getting along with my family again, and I enjoyed life. It was really nice to finally be happy, but problems were now starting to come to the surface at the ministry.

Things never seemed to stay good for very long.

As things began showing up in the ministry that were not consistent with what they said originally, or that were just strange, it produced a lot of questions in me. Because of my place in the ministry though being only a young volunteer, I wasn't allowed to ask questions, so I frowned and tried to accept leaderships rules and ideas which didn't always happen. Submission was a big topic in the ministry, and they frequently taught about how you need to submit to authority -- no questions asked.

My dad was moving higher up in leadership and

he began seeing inefficiencies and bad leadership going on. Whenever he asked a question, it was never fully or directly answered; whenever he tried to make a change, it was turned down. He would come home frustrated and confused. It negatively influenced our life at home. By this time, we had already moved to the country in East Texas where the ministry had bought land, built and moved onto. We had a house five minutes away from campus where they built a large beautiful main office, a chapel for prayer and church services, a cafeteria, a huge warehouse barn, and about 80 houses for the staff. Fortunately, we couldn't fit in any of the campus housing since my family had six kids, four of them teenagers, so we found a place on two-and-a-half acres nearby. After only a year of being out in the country, things went downhill for us with the ministry as the truth was slowly leaking out. We decided the best move would be to leave the missions organization.

In June of 2014, after twelve years of serving as missionaries, we announced our resignation. Because of that, I lost all of the friends that I did have, the normalcy that I had grown up in, and one of the only things I had known. I tried to still be friends with some of the girls on campus, but I was rejected. One of them straight up told me that I was an enemy, and just needed to get used to it. Another told me I couldn't go to her wedding, because it would be too "awkward". No one else would even talk to me...all because we had left. It was somehow the biggest sin we could have committed. I had no one to talk to but my family, and my parents just had a few couples who had also left that they could discuss things with.

I felt so alone.

The truth was out. This place that I had dedicated my life to, and gave all my money, this place where my entire family served and sacrificed, this place...was a cult. It was a complete fake. As my family began talking through what happened, we began noticing things throughout our time there that should have brought up red flags many years prior. Only we were too submissive to see it at the time. This cultish ministry had placed an incredible amount of control on the staff. We were essentially little chess pieces that could only be moved by the big boss president, and if we tried to move on our own, we'd get taken out of the game or excommunicated.

The leaders straight up lied to us. Deceived us. Manipulated us. Emotionally and spiritually abused us. They twisted Bible verses and took them out of context to comply with what they wanted to teach. The president of the ministry had turned himself into a god, a person or deity to be worshipped. People would literally bow down to him, and kiss his ring as a supposed sign of respect over in South Asia. Anyone who left the ministry was a sinner, was not following God anymore, and was to be excommunicated.

The ministry is going to court right now for fraud: over two hundred million dollars unaccounted for in random banks around the world. We found out through leaders over in South Asia, that only 15% of the money donated went to where it was designated, instead of the 100% like the ministry prided itself in saying. We all practically played follow the leader for twelve years of my life, and everyone walked on eggshells trying to make sure they didn't upset the boss, always obeying. It was the most controlling environment I've ever been in, and I wish we'd gotten out sooner.

I felt as if I had given up my life, my time, and my money for nothing. I was extremely mad that I could have been deceived and manipulated for so long. All that money was wasted, on who knows what. I had no one left but my family. I didn't know what I believed anymore. I was having to completely start over with life, goals, and relationships. I couldn't trust anyone -- especially in any type of leadership -- because all I thought of was control, manipulation, and lies. Everywhere I looked, I was reminded of the pain.

I no longer could go past the exit for the campus without instantly having chronic anxiety, fear, and panic attacks. I had thoughts of blowing up the entire ministry to get rid of everyone I hated, and shut down the cult. I couldn't handle life anymore, and fell into a deep depression. A few months later, I was diagnosed with PTSD: Post-Traumatic Stress Disorder. I was confused at first, because I thought only military and first responder personnel could get that diagnoses. But as I will explain in a later chapter, different things can be traumatic for different people, and anyone can develop PTSD.

CHAPTER 4

Shadow of Death

Death is inevitable. Every single person on this earth will at some point in their life breathe their last breath, leaving behind loved ones, family members, and friends. And though it is a reality and something to be expected, the amount of pain that is produced in the ones left behind can turn their life upside down. When someone dies, it can leave a person numb, paralyzed, distraught, angry, sad, and severely grieved. The death can be sudden, or sometimes expected. The very first time that I experienced death was when I was young, and though it was awful, sudden, and emotionally painful, I somehow managed to come to terms with what happened over time. I found a way to distract myself, push back the thoughts and memories, and try to move on. For four years life went on without incident, and I forgot about the pain that I had buried deep down inside.

Then it happened. It was a nice older lady that my brother and sister cleaned for weekly. She was married to someone who worked with my family as a missionary, but she was not doing well with her health. When we received the phone call of her passing peacefully in her sleep, my sister wept. I was only shocked. My mom had had two miscarriages prior to this, and it had been many years since anyone died, but here I was grieving all over again. I wasn't really sure how to respond, but it hurt me to see my sister so sad. A few days later, I went to my first funeral. That was the hardest thing to have witnessed. Even though I wasn't super close to this lady, I still knew her, and that was enough to affect me. I struggled trying to come to terms with the fact that someone had just died, right down the street from where I lived.

Only one month after she passed away, I was hit with another death. A family that we knew from an old church had five kids. We would go over to the park with them, and occasionally have a tea party. We found out through social media, that one of their daughters suddenly died at the hospital from the flu. She was only thirteen years old.

This young girl had been dealing with what seemed to be a normal illness for four days, before her mom decided to take her in to the hospital. On the way there though, she stopped breathing. Once they reached the Emergency Room, nursing staff began lifesaving measures on her. They rushed her into a room, continuing to give CPR, giving her fluids and medications to try and stabilize her body. Her heart was not beating properly to sustain life, her breathing had stopped, and there were many nurses and doctors surrounding her trying to run emergency tests to figure out the cause of her body giving out so quickly. There was no warning that this was going to happen. For ninety minutes there was chaos in the Emergency Room, as everyone worked together as fast as they could to bring this girl back. But they couldn't. After having done everything they possibly could in that time, they finally stopped and called it. This little thirteen year old girl just died from the common flu.

I couldn't understand it. I was just getting over a funeral, and only a few weeks later would have to attend another? What was up with people dying? I started to become afraid in the midst of denying that it ever happened, and then grieving like I've never done before. I went to my first viewing, which was terrifying. To see such a grey body with no soul, haunts you, especially when they're a child. The funeral was beautiful, and heartbreaking at the same time.

Just when I thought things were bad enough, they quickly got worse. Only one month after this little girl died, we had another close family friend whose child passed away. He was the moms sixth child, and was born prematurely with a diagnosis of CHARGE syndrome, which affects the heart, brain, hearing, vision, and more. They weren't sure that he would survive very long, but this little baby kept proving everyone wrong. He had a few surgeries to correct some of the main issues in his body, and seemed to be doing pretty well. I was getting ready to become trained and certified to change his tracheotomy, so I could help out the family if needed. I was excited to see him come home and beat all the odds. He was such a precious little squirt, and I was pretty close with the family too. However, he started quickly declining, and put his parents in a place where they had to decide to take him off life support. He died peacefully in the family's arms, surrounded by love and songs.

My heart was crushed. I went to the viewing, and saw his little lifeless body all dressed up in that casket. It was the second time to see such a sorrowful thing. At the funeral, I couldn't stop weeping. I couldn't deal with this anymore, and thought for sure that someone in my family was next. It became this paralyzing fear that crippled my everyday life. Three people had died within a month from each other, and I couldn't bear the thought of what might happen next.

No one passed on for six months, and then a good friend from the ministry died after a brief battle with cancer. I loved that woman, and had fond memories with her. We worked together, baked cookies, watched movies, and talked about life, so it was difficult to handle. Two years later, another young friend died suddenly after falling off a cliff while hiking with his brother and a few friends. He was almost nineteen years old, and the freak accident stunned most everyone who knew him. It seemed as if life was truly a vapor, and death was always around the corner. Even though I tried to move on, I still battled internally with the concept of death.

I especially experienced this while working as a volunteer firefighter. I started working in a small town in East Texas, in May of 2015, as a volunteer at the fire department. My EMT (Emergency Medical Technician) training had already been done, so the process to get in as a volunteer was a little bit easier. I signed up for a couple shifts for the month, and got excited about starting my career there. Not too long into my time at the department, I had to work two accidents about two weeks apart that would later come back as a traumatizing memory.

The first one was a middle-aged person who fell off a ladder onto concrete. When we arrived, I had to help breathe for them for forty-five minutes in the ambulance until we got to the hospital. It didn't really bother me too much at the time, but hit me a little harder when I found out that the family had pulled life-support a few days later. I tried to suck it up, and told myself that I didn't know them, so it shouldn't affect me. I moved on, and continued focusing on becoming a good firefighter, and learning whenever I could.

Two weeks after that first accident, I got a call to help come cover the station. There had been an accident on the freeway involving three cars -- two of them semi-trucks -- and they needed people at the station to be able to cover any other emergencies that might happen in the area while they were gone. I arrived within fifteen minutes, and waited with two other guys for a call to come in. We finally did get a call, but it was from the guys working the accident.

They requested us to go meet them at the wrecking yard to extricate a deceased person. Instead of blocking traffic for a lot longer to try and get this person out, and since it wasn't an emergency since they had died instantly on impact, firefighters had the tow truck bring the car and body to the wrecking yard, so we could do it safely there. It took us two hours to get this body out in the hundred-degree heat because of how jammed they were in the car. I was asked to help hold the person while they worked on freeing the legs, so I had a very up close and personal experience with a deceased and broken body. Encountering a human in that form, with the absence of life and obvious deformities and trauma, is something intense that you can never forget or unsee.

Afterwards as we were cleaning up and packing up, some of my fellow firefighters asked if everyone was okay or needed any debriefing. One looked at me since I was a newbie and had not experienced anything like this before. I looked up, smiled, and said I was fine. Honestly, I really was. During the time that I was holding that deceased person, I was thinking from a medical standpoint what would be wrong, what I would need to treat, and how I would treat it. That was the only way I could distract myself from the reality, the smell, and the noise of death, and still do my job. I felt proud of myself for having handled that situation, and went home knowing that I was able to handle being a firefighter...at least in that area.

A few months later, though, I began having terrifying memories of these incidents. They were haunting me, and I felt like a failure. I couldn't stop thinking and remembering what I saw, what I heard, and what I felt. Every time anyone else died in my life, all I could see were these people that I had encountered on the job. This constant reminder of death, what it looked like, and what it sounded like, was producing an extraordinary amount of fear. I was permanently scarred by the (now) nine people that had suddenly passed away.

These deaths, coupled with all the confusion and manipulation going on at the ministry, were way too much for me to handle. I had to see a counselor and a psychiatrist in order to get the diagnosis and treatment of PTSD in the summer of 2016. I was traumatized by all these things that I didn't want to affect me, but did anyways. I could no longer see certain things, hear certain sounds, go certain places, or interact with certain people, without having paralyzing fear and anxiety.

Things just weren't the same. I had to be careful about what I did, or where I went. I had to close my eyes and try to take deep breaths whenever I was going by a place with bad memories. I sometimes wished that I could erase those memories and start over in peace. I wanted to stop having these horrifying recollections, because being bothered by them somehow made me feel less of a person. I struggled to control the thoughts and images that plagued my mind, which caused me to panic, to grieve, and to weep.

My life would never be the same.

CHAPTER 5

Allowed to feel

My experience with life, death, and sacrifice, has not been all that normal for someone my age. Things have been heightened, abused, and my emotions have been pushed around like a hockey puck. I am by nature a very sensitive person, so things tend to affect me more than the average person. That can be a good thing because it helps me be more sensitive to other people's emotions and feelings, helping me be empathetic, sympathetic, and encouraging. It can also be something that isn't so good or helpful in other circumstances, like what people say to me could easily affect me in a negative way, and I can be easily traumatized by certain situations that happen in my life.

When experiencing these feelings, I didn't understand what my issue was at first. I thought I was a wimp who couldn't handle anything, maybe some whacko person who let anxiety get to them too much. As I was talking to my counselor and psychiatrist about what was going on, they agreed that I definitely had PTSD. *But how?* I thought. I wasn't in the military, had only worked as a firefighter for nine months as a volunteer, and grew up in a safe Christian family. I thought that there had to be a certain criterion of "extreme trauma" to be diagnosed with that. But as it was explained to me, it made a lot more sense.

You see, it is common to think that only first responders, military members, or people who have experienced sexual or marital abuse, would be the ones to have that diagnosis. And they do. It is a very common diagnoses in those scenarios.[4] However, PTSD can actually affect anyone. Trauma itself can be categorized as "big" or "little."[5] It can affect different people for different reasons. And because everyone thinks and acts different from each other, something that might be traumatic for one person, may not be traumatic for another in the same situation.

---

[4] "Facts about Post-Traumatic Stress Disorder." *MentalHelp.net*, 2006, mentalhelp.net/articles/facts-about-post-traumatic-stress-disorder/. Accessed 20 Aug 2018

[5] Staggs, Sara "Posttraumatic Stress Disorder (PTSD) Symptoms." *PsychCentral*, 2018, psychcentral.com/disorders/ptsd/posttraumatic-stress-disorder-ptsd-symptoms/. Accessed 20 Aug 2018

Trauma can be defined in the dictionary as, "a deeply distressing or disturbing experience," or, "emotional shock following a stressful event or physical injury." For me personally, it was a combination of a lot of things. I had numerous times of emotional shock, and distressing experiences because of having epilepsy as a child, serving at a guilt-filled ministry, suffering from emotional and spiritual abuse, burdened with constant health issues that weren't getting resolved, dealing with constant grief over the loss of friends, and people who died consecutively over a short period of time.

It's amazing how blind I was to the realness and severity of my mental health and the side effects it was having on me. And just like I was clueless for a while, not everyone knows that they have it. I would like to explain to you though, what it feels like to have Post-Traumatic Stress Disorder, ways to deal with it, and how you can help others going through the coping process.

Paralyzing Fear: A huge symptom of PTSD, is a completely paralyzing fear of being near the place, city, street, house, or thing that the traumatic event is connected with. This fear can literally stop your breath in its tracks and cause your heart to race. Being near whatever item, or person, or place that is traumatizing to you brings back all the memories and emotions from

52

that experience, playing it through your brain like a horror movie. Repeatedly making you relive that awful event -- it haunts you. You are constantly on high alert, waiting and terrified that it will happen again. This fear is considered an "avoidance symptom."[6]

Panic Attacks: Going hand and hand with paralyzing fear is panic attacks. Because of the nature of the situation, and the extreme fear that is involved, having a panic attack is almost inevitable. Your body will release a large amount of adrenaline during the flashback, putting you into a fight or flight mode. This increases your heart rate and makes your breathing rapid as if preparing for a fight, or a chance to run. Because you won't be doing either, though, your body doesn't know it and continues to release the adrenaline. It will at that point most likely turn into a panic attack. It will feel like the air is being snuffed out of you at the same time that you are terrified and afraid. The experience is horrifying and overwhelming.

---

[6] "Post-Traumatic Stress Disorder." *National Institute of Mental Health*, 2016, nimh.nih.gov/health/topics/post-traumatic-stress-disorder-ptsd/index.shtml. Accessed 20 Aug 2018

Irrational Thoughts: Although they may seem very legit at the time, you may experience irrational thinking. You may think that everyone is out to get you. You may have thoughts of severe "pay-back" to the person or people that hurt you. Like I mentioned in a previous chapter, I had frequent thoughts and ideas of blowing up the entire place that hurt me. I considered punching and seriously hurting the cult leader as a punishment for his actions. None of that was rational. Another example would be when I experienced all those friends and patients dying, I thought for sure someone in my immediate family was next. I couldn't sleep because I wanted to make sure they were breathing, and would constantly wake up in fear and check to see if my family was still alive. I was being irrational in the situation without realizing it, because to me, it *was* rational. You may also think that you can't trust anybody in your life. Or think that everyone is lying to you, which can't be true because there are good, kind people out there. But nonetheless these are all very real feelings, and definitely normal for someone dealing with PTSD.

Emotions: This issue of dealing with trauma is not an easy thing at all. It can heighten emotions and cause you to become very angry, scared, fearful, sad, and especially depressed. In most all circumstances, depression comes along with Post-Traumatic Stress Disorder. You may feel so sad and alone that you become depressed. You might be angry and frustrated but know that you can't do anything and become depressed. There is an isolating fear that brings depression and anger there with you. A place you can't escape. A place that you fear but can't hide from or avoid.

For those of you who know someone struggling with this disorder, I want to give you some tips of what to do, and what not to do.

The number one thing to NOT do is deny their diagnoses. I once had a friend who straight up told me that I didn't have PTSD because what I experienced was not actually trauma. She would go on to tell me her story of trauma, which was considered worse than what I experienced. I was confused and frustrated, and talked to my counselor about the situation, to which he said her comment was not true at all. I had been diagnosed by professionals, and so don't listen to her.

In all seriousness, trauma no matter how great or how small, is still trauma. And while my friend did go through all that and experience PTSD, she had no right at all to contradict my diagnoses because what I went through was "not as traumatic." It was traumatic for me.

So, whatever you do, please do not contradict the diagnoses, because if you do, it will cause a large amount of distrust towards you and frustrate the already frustrated person. It does not help anything, and could make a lot of things worse, as it feels as if you are insensitive to their feelings and making them feel stupid.

One way to help is to listen. To listen to them share their feelings and their fears. Being there for them is something that every person needs. Don't just do the talking, do the listening. Be sensitive to how they feel, and be understanding. Just because you may not have experienced their exact pain, does not mean you can or should pretend as if it's no big deal: because it definitely is a big deal.

PTSD is painful, and having that constant traumatic memory is terrifying, so it's usually a good idea to let them talk about how they feel because it helps with coping. Validate their feelings by being understanding and compassionate, by telling them that they're feelings are valid and normal. Even though their feelings about life and the people around them may sound exaggerated or incorrect, that is how they see things in the moment and it is normal to feel that way.

Once you have listened to their struggle, and validated their feelings, show them the truth with sympathy. Don't shout it in their face, or say it in a voice of superiority. Kindly and compassionately tell them the truth while validating their feelings. Tell them that you will be there for them and that you're going to get through this together. If they feel like they can't trust anyone, or that everyone is out to get them, gently tell them it's not all true. Explain that there are good people out there that they can trust, and that this is just for a season of time. Tell them the truth about yourself, that you are not going to leave them, that they can trust you, and that you are there to help them through this. Having at least one person they can trust is a huge step in overcoming or coping with PTSD. Companionship is a necessity.

For those of you who are dealing with the effects of Post-Traumatic Stress Disorder right now, here are a few things that helped me.

Talking: Share with someone how you feel. Talk to a friend or close family member about what happened, how it makes you feel, your fears, and your emotions. Do NOT keep it to yourself! It is hard, scary, and traumatizing enough to have to constantly live with it in your head, but don't let it stay there. Talking it out and talking through it takes off some of the burden, and helps with letting go of the situation. If you keep it to yourself, it could eventually cause major issues later on. Do what you can to prevent that and help yourself in this way.

Feel: Crying and being angry or frustrated are acceptable emotional responses. It helps release the internal pain by feeling, being aware of those feelings, and letting them out. If you stuff all your emotions inside, it can cause a huge buildup of pressure mentally and emotionally, which eventually will have to break loose. The problem is it will come out all at one time, out of your control, and you may do things you will regret later. Instead of doing that, learn to be okay with crying or being angry when you have those feelings. They are there for a reason. When angry, be careful though not to act out in rage, since serious damage can come to both you and others. Only be aware of your anger, allow yourself to feel, and don't act on it. Allowing yourself to feel, to have feelings and accept them, is part of the healing process.

Counseling: Going to get counseling is probably the best advice I could offer you. Whether you have experienced someone dying, been abused in any way, seen something horrific that you can't unsee, been in a debilitating accident, grown up in a rough family environment, or any other thing that has traumatized you personally, getting professional help is always a great idea. Don't ever think that you are any less of a person, or not strong enough, if you go to get counseling, because in fact you are doing a really brave thing by taking that step forward towards getting better. Seeing a good counselor is helpful because they are there to listen and give good professional, but practical advice, and to help you in a non-judgmental way that is in a safe, confidential environment. They are trustworthy, and literally there to listen and help others. Going to counseling would give you at least one safe person to talk to, who could give you advice on how to cope with PTSD based on your situation and personality.

Therapy: There are different types of therapy that are used to help people overcome their PTSD. Exposure Therapy is one specific one, which is a type of Cognitive Behavior Therapy that trained and licensed professionals use.[7] I haven't done this type of therapy myself before, but from what I've seen it is a good option as long as it's also recommended by your psychiatrist or counselor.

---

[7] Grohol, John M. "What is Exposure Therapy?" *PsychCentral*, 2016, psychcentral.com/lib/what-is-exposure-therapy/. Accessed 20 Aug 2018

Set Boundaries: There will be certain places, things, or people that will be a traumatic trigger for you, which you need to be aware of. In the beginning it may be best to stay away from those places or things for a period of time. You will need time to process, cope, and recover, and running into that area or those things, will bring back those traumatizing memories and delay the healing and recovery process. So plan your day wisely and set boundaries for yourself. You will not have to do that forever, but during this time, be wise and know that you will eventually have some mental and emotional freedom.

Forgive: If your trauma comes from abuse, or from something that someone else said or did to you, forgiveness may be a good way to be released from the situation. I've never really understood forgiveness until now. I always thought that it meant you were accepting what they did to you as "okay", and that it really wasn't that big of a deal. And I was not about to forgive any person or place that had abused me in my life, because that was not "okay." But recently, I learned that forgiveness is actually letting go. Forgiveness is saying that you are not going to allow them to control your life and your mind anymore. Because until you can forgive them, you will be trapped forever. That circumstance or incident will continue to control you, your mind, and your actions. You must come to a point that you can let go. And forgiving that person is not saying that what they did was right, because it wasn't. What you're saying by forgiving them is that you are moving on and not looking back, not letting them control you anymore. And it can be the most freeing action you can do. You will have to keep forgiving them though, because it's not just a one-time thing. It is easy to fall into that fear and hate again, so it is a constant process, but it's well worth the temporary pain to bring freedom.

As I bring this section to a close, I want to remind you that trauma is trauma, no matter how big or small; the things that are traumatic are different for everybody, and anyone can have Post-Traumatic Stress Disorder. It sucks, it's terrifying, and it's a monster, but it is a real disorder that affects many people. And it is something that can be treated, that can be helped, and that can be beat.

PART 3: DEPRESSION

CHAPTER 6

Battle of the Mind

When I was a teenager, I had dealt with some general depression, but wasn't diagnosed until it had become chronic a few years later. During that time, I would deal with the struggles in life by bottling everything up emotionally, and then finally having a breakdown every 1-2 months. I was never taught how to properly deal with emotions and would usually get sent to my room if I was sad, upset, or angry. Negative emotions or feelings weren't allowed in my house, which didn't set me up for success emotionally, and would, in fact, turn into major issues later on.

As I've mentioned before, I am a very sensitive person. Everything affects me, whether it's in a good way or a bad way. I've often experienced a lot of teasing by other people as a result, hearing everything from "you're just too sensitive" to "you are just making this all up." Needless to say, growing up was difficult. I wasn't allowed to be frustrated, so I stuffed it all inside as long as I could. What no one seemed to understand, though, was that I didn't want to be "sensitive"; I wanted to be considered a strong person.

Things had been going haywire for me for a few months, starting at the beginning of 2016. I had a heat stroke in February during Fire Academy, which completely ended my career as a firefighter, and broke my heart. I became severely depressed, angry, and distant. I couldn't handle anything in life and fought frequently with my parents. Even when I would try to move on and accept what happened, I would end up being tormented by my failure and frustrated that my body would collapse in the middle of my career.

By the time April rolled around, I desperately needed to get out of my parents' house. I decided to drive six hours from East Texas to West Texas to visit a family friend. I was supposed to stay for a few months and possibly get a job, but plans quickly changed as my mental health took a turn for the worse. I lost all value for my own life and struggled with intense thoughts, fears, and anger on a daily basis. My heart raced. My head pounded. I was afraid, hopeless, frustrated, confused...helpless. I didn't know what to do, or if I should even ask for help. I lay in bed crying alone most nights, only hoping that the morning would be better.

On April 5th, 2016, I woke up feeling anxious. Within two hours, I had left my friends' house to go for a walk because the stress of life and the intense emotions I was feeling were too much for me. Maybe walking would help. Maybe my frustrated anxiety would pass. I ended up jogging through an unfamiliar neighborhood with tears streaming down my face, not stopping until I'd come to a dead-end street, with a dry cement-filled creek bed nearly two miles away.

For about forty-five seconds, I contemplated jumping into it head first, wondering if that would be enough to kill me -- or if it would just make life worse.

For some reason, jumping sounded like a good idea, and that terrified me. I'd never had those kinds of thoughts before, and the reality of what I wanted to do shocked me back to the present. I turned around and started walking back the way I came, but I couldn't stop wondering *"what if I had jumped...what would that feel like...would it work...would I still go to Heaven?"*

These strange thoughts kept swirling around my head, and the more I walked, the more overheated I became until I finally had to sit down on a brick wall next to a main intersection. I didn't want to go back to the house. I didn't need to, I told myself. I just needed more alone time. Besides, it's not like I could really face anyone yet, or tell them what was going on in my head.

As I watched the cars speed past me, I wondered what it would feel like to throw myself in front of one of them. *No*, I decided, *that would look too obvious. Plus, it might not even work.* A small part of me screamed "what is going on?". Why was I thinking of suicide? And why did it somehow seem like such a relief? In a way, I guess it was the solution I was looking for: I wouldn't have to deal with life anymore; I wouldn't be depressed or stressed; I wouldn't be labelled "sensitive" again. I would be dead. But I continued to battle my thoughts until I finally got off the wall and started walking back towards the neighborhood.

There was a fire station nearby that looked safe, and I sat underneath a large tree to the side of it. I didn't need to die, I just needed to cool down -- collect my thoughts. I must have dozed off because when I woke my head was pounding, my throat was parched, and my heart rate wouldn't slow down. Someone came and gave me a water bottle; I thought they were an angel, but I found out later it was my friend's son. They had seen me as they drove past, gave me water, and just prayed for me in their car together before driving away, to respect my space. I was dizzy, confused, and depressed. I honestly didn't know what to do. I couldn't process life.

After about an hour and a half of sitting under that tree, one of the firefighters came out and asked if I was okay. I wasn't good at lying, so I told him how I felt. He decided it would be best to have a police officer come talk with me, so he radioed it in. I just kept sitting there, waiting for this to pass. Wanting this insanity to be over. I couldn't understand what was happening.

Five minutes later, I had a police officer crouched by the tree next to me. He was a really nice guy and was trying to understand what was going on. He tried to see if he could help talk me through it, and if we could settle this without an incident. I sobbed as I explained to him how I felt, how I didn't know why, and how I've never felt like this before. I didn't want to go to the hospital, but I had left him no choice. He asked the firefighters on shift to check me out really quick, since I was very lightheaded when I stood up. They took my vital signs and blood sugar, and everything was basically normal, besides a higher heart rate. Of course, in this situation, that was to be expected. I reluctantly got in the back of the cop car, first time ever to do so, and waited to wake up from this nightmare.

On the way to hospital, I had a stress-induced seizure (discussed later on in this book). I could hear what was going on, but could not respond. The police officer pulled up to the Emergency Room entrance and tried to wake me up. He thought I was faking it. After trying to get me out of the car to no avail, he called for a wheelchair. The cop was obviously confused as they wheeled me into a room.

The doctor came quick, because their only thought was that I had overdosed, and had lied to the officer about it. They did blood work and ran numerous tests all which came back normal. I finally came around but couldn't speak. The stress had affected my brain, and now my ability to talk. I did sign language -- which nobody understood -- and eventually started writing down my answers to the thousand questions hospital staff were asking me. My friend came into the room, and I wondered how she found out. Apparently, she had asked the fire-fighters once she realized that I was gone, and they told her where I was. I was thankful to have her there, and yet ashamed to have put her through something like that. She held my hand though as a mother would, talked to me, was with me as I sobbed, and tried to speak truth into my life.

Hours passed as nurses, doctors, social workers, and the police officer discussed what should be done next. They had to find a mental facility that had room for someone at midnight. Arrangements were finally made, and I was once again wheeled to the cop car, with this patient officer who had stayed there the whole time and was now going to transport me. I couldn't believe it. Why had I told the truth? Had I just lied, I could have avoided all this extra crap. We got to the mental facility and he checked me in. I mouthed, "goodbye," and, "I'm sorry," to my friend, while I had tears flowing down my cheeks. These people were taking away everything I had, and I hated it. It was so much worse than I expected.

I had to go through these little checkpoints, filling out paperwork, answering questions, having people mark my body with every scratch and bump that was seen, making sure I wouldn't purposefully hurt myself while I was there. Every door that I was wheeled through was locked, and needed a special fob or key to get into. This was like being in a prison! And how exactly was this supposed to help? I was finally taken to a large area with seating, tables, and a TV; a hallway protruding from one end. I waited there for a room to be ready, and saw at the end of the hallway a girl sitting with her head in her hands, rocking back and forth. She was moaning,

71

and obviously distressed. This sight severely disturbed me. Of course, my room ended up being right across from hers which scared me. I laid on a hard mattress with a thin blanket, and once again cried myself to sleep.

CHAPTER 7

Suicide

The next morning, I was woken up by the facility staff for the normal routine: vital signs, then everyone lining up for breakfast. I could finally talk, but I was still too weak to walk so I had to use a wheelchair. Everyone stared at me as I wheeled myself around. I didn't know what to think. I was trapped in this place with nineteen other people, who all had different ailments ranging from suicidal attempts, to depression, to anxiety, and bipolar disorders. I felt angry, and hated the feeling of being imprisoned. I wanted to get out of this wretched place.

Vitals were done, and now everyone was lining up to go eat. There were staff "guards" in the front and back of the line who led us out of our quarters to the dining hall. No one was allowed to go back without an escort, so everyone stayed until all finished having breakfast. The whole rest of the day was boring. Just sitting around, some watching television, some on the phone during specific calling hours, asking for coloring pages, talking to the other patients, taking a nap, doing whatever you could to pass the time. Occasionally there would be an "activity" time, where everyone went outside into the courtyard for fresh air, drawing, or playing outdoor games. There were always at least two staff people out there keeping an eye on everyone. It never lasted very long, maybe about five minutes, and then we all had to line up to go back inside.

Night time came around, and I was so depressed I didn't think I could handle it anymore. This placed sucked, had nothing to offer, and didn't help at all. I was mad at everyone, at everything, and at life. Visitors were only allowed twice a week, so trying to survive with hardly any outside contact seemed impossible. I couldn't even call anyone, except twice a week for ten minutes. I went to bed that night with conflicted thoughts, lots of questions, confusion, and anger. Why would anyone stay alive if just to experience this? And especially, why the heck was I the one having to be put through it?

My head was spinning, and I had just had enough. Suicide was going to be my way out. The staff wouldn't notice because my door was almost shut, and they didn't come in very often anyways. I was sure I could finally pull this off, and be in peace forever.

I quietly grabbed the sheet that was on me, and slowly slipped it around my neck. It was a slow process, because my bed creaked, and I also didn't want them to hear any rustling noise. I wrapped it around twice and tied it as tight as I could. It wouldn't get as tight as I wanted it to, because it was wadded up in a thick mass. I tried cinching it tighter and stretching my arm out to constrict it more. It worked better, though not great, and I laid there shallowly breathing. My eyes were closed, my heart and head pounding, asking for oxygen. I wondered how painful it would be to take my last breath of air. I laid on that hard mattress, with a sheet wrapped tightly around my neck for about twenty minutes. The color was slowly draining out of my face, as my lungs cried out for more air. I could feel them burning. I was trying to slow my breathing down to a stop and got very close. I was starting to get quite fatigued and became eerily relaxed as I realized I was succeeding.

Suddenly out of nowhere, I envisioned my two youngest brothers, and wondered how they would find out, and if they would understand. The littlest was only three years old and had always been my little buddy. The thought of them being sad because of something that I had done hurt me more than anything else at that time.

I loosened the sheet around my neck and gasped for air. My eyes watered, and I quietly called for help. It took the staff a few minutes to hear me, because I didn't have enough strength to call very loudly. When they did come in though, they knew right away what had happened. With the sheet still partly around my neck, the ends twisted and wrinkled, and my face white, it was obvious. The staff lady called for the nurse, and all of a sudden, I had four mental health staff in my room. They started taking my vitals, and eventually processes in my body began to regulate. I was able to replenish most of my oxygen within a few minutes, and was quickly placed in a front room with a guard, and no sheets or blankets. Whenever the air conditioning came on, shivers ran up and down my spine. Yeah, I deserved this, but it sure wasn't pleasant.

I didn't sleep much that night and felt rather breathless. It had been quite eventful, and I wasn't sure if I was sad, or happy, or ashamed. I had someone following me around for the next three days, day and night, no matter what I was doing -- even the bathroom door had to be cracked open. The first morning after my suicide attempt, the staff made sure that the doctor got around to evaluating my situation first. It took over an hour to get my health history, run a few tests, and discuss what meds would be best for me. I felt a small spark of hope for the first time, since it appeared that someone cared and wanted to help by getting me on the right medicines. At least that was a start!

I ended up staying in that mental health hospital in West Texas for almost three weeks, trying to get my mind put back together, and become more stabilized with medication. I hobbled out of there still feeling very weak, but better than when I had first come, and glad to finally be free.

It didn't last too long though. My dad came to pick me up from my friends' house, and brought me back home. Everyone there seemed different. They all looked sad, and practically had question marks written all over their face. I tried to get into a mental rehabilitation facility, but they were way too expensive, and not many of them even had space. I was becoming more and more frustrated as I tried to do research to find the help and therapy that I knew I needed, but nothing I tried was working. I was failing when I was trying to do something right. I did get into one mental rehab facility, only to be wrongly kicked out after a few days of being there. Life put me into a severe depression again soon after that experience. I thought I was obviously useless, helpless, and hopeless, and that life was just never meant to get better.

June 5th, 2016, I started crumbling emotionally. I stayed home from church and honestly tried my best to do the "right things" to come out of my severely depressed state with suicidal tendencies. I didn't want to be suicidal. I didn't really want to end my life, but that's where my mind was going. I called a friend. I went on a walk. I watched a comedy. But I couldn't shake the feeling of wanting to kill myself. For hours of torture, I battled with my own mind.

My parents came home, and I had to plead with them to take me to the hospital. I couldn't trust myself, with so many possible ways to kill myself lying around. After discussing it and crying for thirty minutes, my parents finally agreed to take me in. I was in the hospital for many hours waiting for guidance and help. There was a security officer in the doorway the entire time, due to my situation. Finally, I got word that I was being transferred by ambulance to a mental facility that had space, about an hour away. I had conflicting thoughts about going to another mental facility. Yes, the other one did help a little bit, but it also was awful most of the times because of the loneliness, lack of outside social interactions, and the feelings of being imprisoned. I wondered how this place could actually help me and if it would be different from the first.

I was transferred that night and didn't sleep well. Then the whole next day was a wash. The staff workers sat behind a desk, that had glass windows surrounding it, all the way up to the ceiling. They never interacted with the patients, asked how they were doing, or if they needed anything. Instead, you would only see them if it was medication time, or meal time. I wondered why I was in a place that could care less if you were alive or dead, with people who didn't look out for others? This was ridiculous. By June 7th, the following day, I had had enough of this crap. They didn't care about life, or if other people lived, so why should I? Pulling off suicide would be easy. The staff were usually behind their desks during the day, so "taking a nap" would be a simple enough disguise.

I went in my shared room and pretended to sleep. I was done being alive, feeling stupid and depressed. I decided to retry strangling. I did the same slow process, wrapping the sheet around my neck and tying it as tight as possible. Circulation and color was draining from my face, as the oxygen was being depleted from my brain. It was slowly working yet again. My breathing became less as I waited for that final moment, with no fear at all. Suddenly, staff were in my room after they had realized that they weren't doing their job by keeping an eye on the patients, when they noticed the unusual amount of fabric by my neck. The staff came and quickly unwrapped the sheet, calling for more help. I had been caught and was not at all happy about it.

As the air once again came back into my lungs and re-oxygenated my brain, the mental health staff moved me into a separate room. I would spend the next two days with no sheets, a mattress on the floor, the lights on 24/7, and a guard to watch me. There was no trying that again! I saw the doctor, but got no good help. I also had my physical boundaries violated by one of the staff workers while having another stress-induced seizure, so I checked out of that place against medical advice. After leaving, I eventually raised enough money to go to a second mental rehab facility. It wasn't until then though, that I finally learned the value of my life, and also how to cope with depression.

CHAPTER 8

Validation

As you may have realized, my journey with depression has been pretty intense. It affected me to the point of me trying to take my life, not only once, but twice. It has overtaken me, many days in each year, and is something I still struggle with quite frequently. Depression is not really something that will just "go away." It's a constant battle and process that takes place every single day. It is a dark place, that needs light and understanding.

So, in this chapter, I want to explain to you what it feels like to be depressed, and a few things that have helped me overcome this mental issue.

Feeling Alone: One of the biggest issues in regards to depression, is the fact that it is a very lonely place. When you feel depressed, you might feel that you are the only one going through this; that nobody understands; that you are stupid (since "nobody else" feels this way); or that there is no one who can help you through it. To be honest with you, it's hard to be convinced otherwise. These are *very* real thoughts that are easy to believe, and hard to disprove when you're going through this, which is unfortunately the reality of this mental illness. Even though depression affects eighteen million adults in a given year and is the primary reason of suicide,[8] the severe feeling of loneliness that is experienced when going through this makes a person believe that they are truly the only one.

Lack of Motivation: When you feel depressed, it actually drains you physically. People won't have any energy or motivation to do simple tasks like getting out of bed, doing laundry, getting dressed, and sometimes, even eating. It is like a sickness that overtakes your body, to the point that everything hurts. It is easier for a person who is depressed to stay in their room, in bed, and not interact with anyone outside of that room, then to do normal daily tasks. Why is it so hard? Because even though it may not seem like it, it is physically and emotionally taxing on the body. It causes lack of concentration, no interest in doing anything, and

---

[8] "Depression Facts." *Hope for Depression Research Foundation*, 2018, hopefordepression.org/depression-facts/. Accessed 21 Aug 2018

severe lack of energy.[9] They are already struggling to cope with the intense feelings and thoughts that are in their mind, and adding "activities" such as getting dressed can cause the brain to freak out...or at least that's what it feels like.

Emotions: Strong and often unwanted feelings can be present during times of depression. Sadness, anger, and fear are the three that have been strongest for me. There seems to be no way to get rid of these emotions or feelings, which can therefore cause agitation. It is extremely hard to deal with and process such strong emotions, and these types of feelings can also be a huge factor in becoming worn out. Just being sad can cause a great amount of fatigue. It can also cause general weakness and lethargy. The emotions and feelings weigh you down to the point of a breakdown, and can cause a sort of panic due to the intensity of the feelings.

Short-Sightedness: The depression that a person is experiencing can cloud their vision in life. It becomes a big black hole that they seemingly can't get

---

[9] "What is Depression?" *WebMD*, 2017, webmd.com/depression/guide/link-to-other-mental-illnesses#2. Accessed 21 Aug 2018

out of, where there is no light, or anything to live for. It does not enable them to see past the present conditions or have any hope for a future. The lack of positivity, and constant negativity does not help the situation, but is extremely difficult to change, when in that state of mind. Being positive usually feels like an impossibility, and therefore can sometimes produce anger, feelings of stupidity, and sadness.

Dealing with an issue like depression is often a daunting task. Not everyone experiences all of these symptoms at once -- or as strongly -- but generally they will experience some with varying intensities. Since each person is different, it can sometimes be difficult to know if you or a friend is struggling with depression. Some people don't want to talk about it for fear of rejection, shame, guilt, or taunting/teasing. I personally didn't talk about my feelings and depression for those reasons, and the fact that I didn't think anyone would understand. There is that sense of loneliness that actually comes in the way of being able to get help when you need it.

As I have journeyed through this battle of severe depression for the last three years, I have come to learn what helps, and what hurts more. Here are a few of my own conclusions.

Friends: The biggest help that I have had in overcoming depression, were the friendships that I've had. You absolutely *need* at least one or two close friends who will be there for you, that you can trust, and be honest with. You need support and backup, because you can't do this alone. If you have a friend or family member that is dealing with depression, please be that friend. Be there for them. Listen more than you speak. Be understanding. Validate their feelings. Validation is a huge component to helping them through their issues. When I was dealing with depression, it took me a long time to find someone to validate my feelings, tell me I wasn't crazy, encourage me, and especially just listen. Once I found that person, my life began to change for the better. It is more frustrating to hear that "you're wrong," or, "that's not true," then to have someone tell you that what you're feeling, and how you're acting in response, is understandable. Don't rebuke them. They need gentle reminders and encouragements. So watch what you say, and be a friend.

Write: One of the things that helped me get through the rough spots was to write down a few beautiful things each day. I made a list and would add to it every evening. It ranged from sleeping, to my favorite food, to a quality I appreciated. Most anything in life can be considered beautiful. Doing that helped me focus on sweet thoughts even for just five minutes. It brought a small ounce of positivity that grew as I wrote. I can't say it was easy at first, because it wasn't. It took a little while to get used to and be okay with, but once I had a routine, it became easier and easier, until it was actually enjoyable. It helped me see that there is more to life than the negativity I was seeing; that I could find beauty even in the little things. Journaling was another thing that helped as well. Being able to get my thoughts out on paper was helpful in processing my feelings and emotions.

Counseling: Sometimes we all need some professional help, and that's okay. I was always afraid to see a counselor because I thought they would just report me to a mental facility, or tell me all the things I was doing wrong, and about how much of an idiot I was. Boy, was I wrong! I have been consistently seeing a counselor for a year, and it has been a completely different experience than I ever thought possible. Everything you say is 100% confidential -- thanks to United States laws -- so your story won't be broadcasted throughout the world. If you don't have a friend to talk to, seeing a counselor on a regular basis would be very helpful. I have friends that I can talk to, and a counselor who listens, and both offer any advice they can. It has been a great combination for my particular situation that I highly recommend. Being able to talk to someone who is professionally trained to help people going through different psychological issues, in a way that is tailored to each individual's need, is a huge benefit to our society. Grab a hold of that opportunity!

Exercise: Many people mentioned this to me, that exercise is a great way to overcome depression and even suicidal thoughts. The natural reaction (endorphins) your body has towards exercise, boosts your "happy chemicals," aka the dopamine receptors in your brain, making you feel really good. I have really enjoyed running 5K's and have done seven 5K's and one 10K in the last three years. It gives you something to do, to train for, to feel accomplished in. You can run, jog, or walk, but I must say that crossing that finish line in whatever place you're in is extremely satisfying and rewarding! Personally, it gives me the confidence that I can actually accomplish something. There are virtual 5 & 10K's that you can do from home, which is nice and still rewarding. Just start walking, jogging, lifting weights, or bike riding. Any type of exercise like that is great for your mental health. You don't have to race though, because playing sports are awesome, too. Volleyball, basketball, tennis, baseball, swimming, or anything else active. Just get moving.

Medicine: Seeing a psychiatrist and getting some help medically is very helpful. It is not a horrible thing like you may think. I know from experience that finding the right medicine that worked for me helped to eliminate some of the depressive thoughts and change my mood in a more positive way. There are lots of different medications out there and working with a psychiatrist to figure out which one works could really change your life.

Religion: I do realize that not everyone is religious, but I do want to say that I consider myself a Christian, a believer of Jesus Christ, and that knowing Him has been an encouragement to me during these trying times. I didn't always believe in Him and had many times when I doubted or struggled. But having God in my life, knowing that He cares for me, and is working my situation out for His good (and mine too), has put some hope into such a dark time. If you are religious, praying is a helpful idea. Telling God how you feel -- even if you're angry -- will release some of the burden you are carrying, and free you at least a little bit. I also like to read the *Jesus Calling* book by Sarah Young. It has daily encouragements from Jesus' perspective, and helps lift me up when I am struggling. It isn't a cure all, but it sure does help.

Talk: If any of you are currently struggling with suicidal thoughts, the most important thing I could recommend is that you talk about your feelings to somebody, whether a friend you trust, or even a person on the suicide hotline. I know for me, talking was the last thing I wanted to do, and hated even the thought of it. But once I did talk to someone about my immediate thoughts, it helped me to rationalize them and come to a conclusion after a period of time that my thoughts were actually backwards. That in fact people did need me and that I was wanted, even though it was hard to see sometimes. You see, the two stories I mentioned were not the only times I was suicidal. It has happened numerous times, but now I know how to best deal with it. If you call a friend right away, and talk to them for a while, you will possibly start to feel better emotionally. In fact, suicidal thoughts don't usually last for hours at a time, so please be encouraged that it does get better. If you don't have a friend, call the Suicide Hotline at: 1-800-273-8255, and a friendly person will talk to you. You don't need to worry about being "taken in" because they are only there, and trained to help you over the phone 24/7. It is confidential, and they just want to help you get through that time.

As I bring Part 3 to a close, I want to encourage each one of you who are reading this to learn to listen. Most of us (I used to as well) like to talk about ourselves whenever we can, without really giving the other person a chance to speak. However, being a listener could actually save someone's life. So listen, and be an encourager. Be one who validates others feelings. Be a light in this dark and captive illness by being a friend. By being *there*.

Do not think of depression as something that they can control, because that's not how it works. It's *not* their fault. It is literally an electrical error in the brain. Do not treat them as stupid, or irrational, but rather show them love, respect, and honor. Show them how valuable they are. That they are worth it. You can change the world, one person at a time.

PART 4: SELF-HARM

CHAPTER 9

Emotional Pain

While I was finally in a really good mental health recovery program after my two suicide attempts, I stayed with some friends nearby. The program lasted a month, and though it was very emotional and hard, it was good for me. However, towards the end of my time there, I had the strangest urges that I had never felt before. I suddenly wanted to hurt myself. My mind was racing with these new thoughts and with trying to figure out what to do with them. The temptation was strong, and I couldn't handle the anxiety, so I did something I've never done before: I purposely cut myself. I got the lid of a can, tensed up, and cut my arm, not knowing what to expect, only trying to relieve the anxiety. The crazy part was that the pain felt good. It was relieving to do, so I did it a couple more times before throwing the lid out and dabbing my bloodied arm with a paper towel.

I couldn't believe it. Yeah it kind of hurt, but in

some way was a release of the anger and emotional pain I had felt for so long. I went into my room shocked at what had just happened and started shaking from the fear of someone finding out.

The next morning before I left for the program, I did it again. This time with a serrated knife. I cut myself a few more times, and tried to go deep, though it was a bit hard. After a little while I stopped so I could clean up, and make sure I wouldn't be late. I also made sure to wear a sweatshirt in the facility to cover up the fresh wounds. Thankfully, the air conditioning was running full blast, so it was needed anyways. I was nervous all day and tried not to show it. One of the last sessions we had for the day was just an open discussion on how we were doing. I was terrible at lying -- though sometimes I wished I was better at covering things up -- and I burst into tears. With a shaky voice, I told everyone what I was struggling with, and what I had done, not sure how all the people would respond.

They thanked me for sharing, were very comforting, and were trying to show me that cutting was not a good way to cope with my mental anxiety and pain. They said that I needed to have a different way to show strength. After the session was over, I was pulled aside by a nurse and my psychiatrist who told me that I had to promise I would stop cutting right away, or they would by law have to report me to a mental health facility and I wouldn't be able to finish the last week of the rehab program. At first, I said that I couldn't promise because I didn't think I could keep it. But they kept reinforcing that they would have to report me and would have to check my arm the next day to make sure I hadn't cut myself any more, and I wasn't about to be put back in a mental hospital again. I reluctantly obeyed for the rest of that week and completed the program.

Because I was forced to stop cutting, the urge finally went away after a while and I began to move on with my life with visible scars from the past. It wasn't until about a year later that I started struggling again with daily suicidal thoughts, chronic depression, and major anxiety issues. I was having to talk to my few friends every day, telling them they were going to have to give me a good reason not to kill myself. They would talk me through that time until the suicidal thoughts passed for the day and continually reminded me that they couldn't live without me. They told me that I was somehow loved and valued, and they would become isolated and depressed if I took my life. And every day we would go through the same routine because of my strong feelings to die. My friends were trying to get me to see a counselor for a while, but I wouldn't have it. After a few weeks of this constant issue I decided to secretly try something else.

I thought that if the people I knew really did care about me and wanted me alive then I would cope with these feelings, intense thoughts, and emotional agony, in a different way. So, I decided to start cutting again. It felt so good and was the only thing that could relieve the severe anxiety, mental pain, and feelings that I was a nobody, without actually ending my life. It was my escape, and was to me a sign of strength. At this time, I was living with a sweet godly family that I knew and trusted while I tried to get my life together with handling a job at a hospital doing food service. The family knew I was struggling, but didn't know the extent of it. Work was stressful, friendships were stressful, finances were being drained, health was not so great, so yeah, I didn't want to live anymore.

Once I had decided to start cutting again I couldn't stop. It was addictive and extremely hard to extinguish. I had forgotten how great it felt until I started it back up after having been okay for almost a year.

I snuck into the kitchen after everyone had gone to bed and grabbed a medium-sized serrated knife from the knife block. I quietly crept back into my room, closed the door, and went into the bathroom to fulfill my plan. Ahh! I was finally able to relieve the stress of the day. Feeling the pain and seeing the blood somehow had a calming effect on my mind. I began believing that cutting was a sign of strength because I was able to get through all that pain, and it was helping me not kill myself. Giving me the strength to live. I thought the scars would later show a tale of jaw-dropping strength and perseverance.

After a few nights in a row of cutting, I had my friends over for dessert and a backyard campfire with my host family. It was a last-minute idea that the mom had suggested, and I was scrambling around trying to help her get things ready while at the same time trying to hide my arm. I had done a good job of hiding it up until then since I had to wear long-sleeves for work and assumed I could fool my friends too by just keeping my hands to myself and facing certain directions. I didn't want to wrap it up, because that would be too obvious that something had happened.

So, I pretended to be happy when they came over and did my best hosting them while being completely stressed out on the inside. Keeping this a secret was harder than I expected. We got through the night and I did my now usual routine of cutting at my arm with a knife before bed. Seeing the blood would strangely make me smile. Of course, I would always thoroughly wash the knife by hand afterwards and put it in the dishwasher so as to still be sanitary. I didn't want to be *that* disgusting and irresponsible.

The next morning one of my friends texted me, and asked why I was doing "that". I played stupid and asked what he was talking about. He replied with, "you know what I'm talking about. We all saw the cuts on your arm last night." He was extremely concerned and confused as to why I would purposefully hurt myself. I explained how they didn't want me to kill myself, so this was my only other way to cope with my thoughts and feelings. I tried to make it sound like it was no big deal because to me it wasn't. It was something I was proud of and yet at the same time I was afraid of what others might think. My friend told me I needed to stop cutting, because it wasn't a better option. But I couldn't. It was too satisfying a feeling to stop. Every now and then I would switch it up and use a safety pin to poke into my arm as far as I could, and a few times hit nerves or major blood vessels. I also used the lid of cans, but that was a little harder to effectively use.

As days went on and the scars got bigger and multiplied, it became harder and harder to hide. I was constantly wearing jackets or my long-sleeved work clothes around the house, but it was the beginning of May in Texas, so the heat was really getting to me. I only had three good friends at the time who all knew about it and were trying their best to change my train of thought.

One evening I was hanging out with one of them and he asked if he could see it. I reluctantly said yes, and he could instantly tell that the wounds were becoming infected. He said that I needed to cover it up and not take the bandage off, because if I cut anymore it would get a lot worse. I did wrap it after having argued with him about it for a while but couldn't handle the anxiety by the next morning. I quickly unwrapped the bandage and began relieving the stress by cutting again. My friends were all three texting me at the same time begging me to stop, but I was mad and panicky. So, a new plan formed, and they said if I absolutely had to harm myself then I had to take care of it and keep it clean afterwards with Neosporin and a wrap. I thought that was a decent deal, so I agreed.

The problem with wearing a white noticeable gauze wrap around my forearm, was that it was impossible to keep a secret now. So I made up a believable story that would later go along with the scars when I took the bandage off. I came home from the pool one day sporting the new wrap on my arm and said that I was bending over to pick up something I had dropped, when a dog came running over and scratched my arm. The dog was trying to climb up me because it got so excited around people. Those I told seemed to believe me and that was what I would tell everyone who asked, for the next few months.

I did end up seeing a counselor after a while and at that point was already experiencing extreme pain on the wound site, with tingling in my fingers. Cutting was starting to become too painful and I was frustrated. To me, that meant I wasn't strong enough anymore and was becoming a wimp. It was suggested by my friends and the counselor, that I go see a doctor, because my self-inflicted injury was visibly infected. Sure enough, the Emergency Room doctor had to put me on strong antibiotics and pain meds, explaining to me how important it was to stop cutting.

This was a huge eye opener for me, because they were talking about how if I continued I may have to have my arm amputated, or I could die if the infection got in my bloodstream and spread throughout my body. After another week or two of slowing down the frequency I finally stopped cutting, frustrated with myself and not at all concerned about what I had just done. I just had never expected it to become this bad with such serious consequences. All of this, because of the mental and emotional pain that tormented my mind each and every day.

CHAPTER 10

Understanding

Self-harm is unfortunately a very common problem throughout America, and is often a silent struggle. Upwards of thirty-five percent of Americans deal with self-harm, with cutting being the most common. It affects mainly teenagers and college-age students, but adults also suffer from its grip. Most, if not all of the people who purposely hurt themselves, don't talk about their issue to others...at least not for a while. Sometimes no one ever knows. It is a hidden struggle that they don't want to discuss. If you haven't dealt with it yourself it may be hard for you to wrap your mind around this concept of self-harm, so I would like to help by explaining what it's like, why people do it, and how you can help.

The process of cutting has a strange and satisfying effect on the brain. When the first thought comes to mind, it comes with a burst of adrenaline and a panic or anxiety that is not relieved until it has felt the pain or seen the blood. Self-harm is coupled with depression and anxiety and can be a result in addition to suicidal thoughts.

When someone is depressed -- as I mentioned earlier in this book -- one of the biggest symptoms is the feeling of loneliness. They may feel like nobody understands, or even cares. That may lead the thought process down a path of low to no self-esteem, hating themselves and not caring what happens to them. Cutting, burning, or running into things to cause bruising, are just a few ways that people do self-harm to help with coping, relieve anger, and calm anxiety. Some people hurt places on their body that can be covered up by clothing like their thighs. Others may do their shoulders, arms, or legs and make up a believable story or cover it up with a jacket and pants no matter the season.[10]

It is an easy thing to get away with and do in secret. And because of the calming effect it has on the brain it is sometimes seemingly impossible to stop. For

---

[10] "Self-Injury (Cutting, Self-Harm, or Self-Mutilation)." *Mental Health America*, 2018, mentalhealthamerica.net/self-injury. Accessed 21 Aug 2018

example, people can have an addiction to most anything: TV, alcohol, smoking, eating excessively, and so on. Well, self-harm is also considered an addiction. It is pleasurable, there is a constant need or desire for it, and it satisfies the craving or anxiety. Once you've started it's hard to stop, just like any other addiction.[11]

For me, I thought it was an honor to hurt myself and that people would look up to me with respect because I was a strong person, able to handle anything. It was secretly a sign of strength. The reason it was a secret was because I didn't know if other people thought of it that way. Honestly, I kind of made that up to give myself permission to do what I felt I needed to do. It sounded good and I hated my body anyway, so it was a win-win in my head. I began believing that lie, until it became solidified in my mind, and cutting was then okay only when I was by myself. I didn't desire the pain on other people at all, I only wanted it on me. I felt I deserved pain and thought that if I could build up a tolerance to it

---

[11] Hendriksen, Ellen "4 Surprising Facts About Cutting and Self-Harm." *Quick and Dirty Tips*, 2015, quickanddirtytips.com/health-fitness/mental-health/4-surprising-facts-about-cutting-and-self-harm. Accessed 21 Aug 2018

then maybe people would stop saying I was so sensitive. I really did want to be noticed for strength in people's eyes, I just didn't know how to do it. So, I suffered in silence and relieved the mental pain by inflicting physical pain.

Not everyone thinks like me, though. Some people do self-harm because they hate themselves or how they look, or they don't care anymore. Some do it as a punishment to themselves because they are not who they want to be. Some people do it to gain a sense of belonging, or to stop the bad feelings they are having. Mainly though, people do self-harm to deal and cope with the emotional pain that they are experiencing. It's ironic but true that inflicting physical pain distracts the brain from the constant tormenting of emotional pain that nobody can put a Band-Aid on, thus providing temporary relief.

Mental and emotional pain is one of the worst feelings especially since it's hard for others to understand, so there's no outside support and they must constantly live with their thoughts with no escape. It oftentimes seems hopeless and disheartening. Cutting, burning, or bruising can be that way of escape. That way to temporarily distract themselves from the pain of their thoughts or mind.

These ideas may come as a shock to you if you've never experienced these thoughts yourself, but it is the reality of self-harm and it's widely done in secret. Ways that you can help the situation is to not freak out or show extreme disapproval when you find out. It is essential that you be understanding. Showing criticism or disgust can cause distrust and more frustration, which is something they don't need and is not beneficial in any way. Even though you may disagree with their actions, be calm and understanding, being there for the person. Showing disapproval or threatening to stop them, could cause another act of self-harm because of the stress you have caused.[12] Make sure to not ask them to describe how they hurt themselves, because that can also be another trigger to do it again.

Essentially, there's not a whole lot you can do to prevent it from happening, but you can influence the frequency of it in a positive way by being an encourager and friend. One suggestion I have is to send a daily

[12] "Self-Harm." *Mind for Mental Health*, 2016, mind.org.uk/information-support/types-of-mental-health-problems/self-harm/for-friends-and-family/#.W34Yr5NKjyU. Accessed 22 Aug 2018

encouraging text to the person you know is struggling with self-harm. It may help to boost their self-esteem and to know that they have a good friend that doesn't judge them. Lastly, suggest to them that seeing a counselor would help them have someone confidential and non-judgmental to talk to about what they're struggling with. Don't force them to go, but kindly suggest it and maybe even send them a name and number of a counselor for them to call.

If you are reading this, and struggle with self-harm yourself, I would encourage you to try some of these suggestions, a few of which I wish I had done myself.

Exercise: When you are feeling that rush of adrenaline, that anxiety, and that urge for pain, try and exercise. Running, lifting weights, using the treadmill, doing planks, push-ups, or crunches, can be an outlet for the adrenaline and yet still feel that physical pain only in a little different of a way. You don't have to do it for super long, just try a little bit each time and see if it helps at all after a while. It should at least bring that rush of adrenaline down and not have the feeling be as intense.

List: Make a list of encouraging things about yourself and even decorate it if you want. I did this, and it at least gave me something positive to look at, decreasing the frequency of cutting. A few of the things I wrote on there are:

- I am strong.
- I am an overcomer.
- I have value.
- I am beautiful
- I have purpose.
- I am awesome.

It helps to build up your self-esteem with this because usually it is depleted to begin with. So encourage yourself and then maybe you could even say one of those things to someone else to encourage them. Just doing that can really make you feel good and put a smile on your face!

Set Limits: When trying to cope with the things that you battle in your mind, sometimes you really can't help but cut, burn, or bruise. And honestly, it could do more harm than good to try and stop doing that cold turkey if you've already started. So, start limiting yourself to how many cuts you can make a day or a week; how many bruises you give yourself; or how many times you burn. That helped it not become excessive for me but still fulfilled that urge. Because of how constant and frequent I was doing self-harm, I limited myself to two cuts and two pokes daily which was quite a bit less than what I was doing before. From then on, it became easier to slow down and lesson the amount because it wasn't as exciting anymore. So, if you can't stop cold turkey, set limits and gradually do it less and less as time goes on. The goal is to not have to do self-harm for fulfillment and to use other activities as outlets for your anxiety and adrenaline.

Counseling: Going to see a counselor really helped me find fulfillment in healthier things and gave me someone safe that I could tell my problems to. It helps to have a person you can talk to, that won't judge you, threaten you, or gossip about you. They usually are very understanding and give some helpful tips from a professional standpoint. Seeing a counselor helped me process through my thoughts and find other coping skills for the emotional pain.

The one thing to remember when dealing with self-harm is that it is actually quite dangerous. While doing it myself, I knew that it wasn't the best idea to be purposely inflicting myself with wounds, but I didn't realize the extent of harm that it could do to my body. I mean, I get cuts and scrapes all the time and I'm fine...so what's the big deal? Well, it wasn't a big deal until I started losing feeling in my fingers periodically and having a tingling sensation. My arm began burning whenever I went swimming, or even took a shower. Pus would ooze out when the wounds got wet and grossed people out. The area became very red and somewhat swollen.

After a month of cutting I was forced to go to the hospital because I was feeling feverish, nauseous, weak, and shaky, and I ended up having to quit my job. The doctor was extremely concerned because of the severe infection that I had. And honestly, it's a shock and a miracle that I didn't have to have my arm amputated. I also could have lost my life if the infection had reached my bloodstream.

So, remember the dangers when you are thinking of participating in the act of self-harm. Know that there are severe consequences if you do and that it would be best to start with a different coping method. Please know that there are other people besides you who struggle with this; you are not alone. And there are many resources out there that can help you through this time, so take advantage of that. Don't give up, whatever you do, and keep fighting through this. You are strong!

PART 5: CONVERSION DISORDER/PNES

CHAPTER 11

Mysterious Symptoms

While growing up as a teenager, I was kind of an abnormal one. I had multiple random health issues that were unsolvable, would eventually just "clear up" on its own, and then a completely different medical issue would quickly occur soon afterwards. It was a constant battle and going to the doctor to hear them say nothing was wrong with me became a frustrating norm. No one could tell me what was going on even though I had these serious symptoms.

One of the first major issues came in 2015. I had a job working at a grocery store as a courtesy clerk and helped bag groceries, do some of the front-end work, and take customers out to their car to help unload their bags. It wasn't super stressful, but I was constantly on my feet and ran around making sure everyone got helped. It was tiring, but I did it. I had worked for a few months and felt like I was doing well at my job.

As time went on, I started having severe allergic reactions to smells. I was already allergic to many different foods and had an Epi-Pen with me, though I had never had to use it. The only severe reaction I'd had to a smell was when I was around cigarette smoke or strong perfumes. Other than that, it was only when I ate something that I was allergic to that I would react with hives, a migraine, nausea, shortness of breath, or fatigue. I would deal with whatever symptoms I had, though it was never enough to require the use of an Epi-Pen.

The first time I had a severe reaction to something I didn't eat, happened while at work. I was helping to load twenty-five bags of deer corn in the back of a customer's pick-up truck when a few minutes into the ordeal I began having trouble breathing. I was trying to not show it and finish up, but it was difficult since I was beginning to wheeze. My airway was getting tighter and tighter. I finished loading with a smile and ran back inside to the break room to get my inhaler. I didn't know if it was an asthma attack or an allergic reaction to the corn. The inhaler didn't work, so I used one of my Epi-Pen's for the first time. After a little while, it kind of helped -- though not all the way -- and I slowly closed out my shift that night struggling to breathe.

However, that was only the beginning. From then on, about every other day that I worked I had a reaction to a smell. Sometimes it was bread from the bakery that I was bagging. Sometimes it was a pizza pocket or wings that were being heated up in the break room. Whenever it hit though, it hit fast. I started wearing a painter's mask all the time to protect myself from the fumes. I was constantly having to buy more Epi-Pen's, which cost a fortune -- almost four hundred dollars for a pack of two.

In just a matter of about three weeks, I went to the hospital over ten times; whether by ambulance, or by my mom driving me. The Epi-Pen's weren't really working anymore, and I daily struggled to breathe. It was almost as if my lungs were weakening with every reaction. At one point, I breathlessly begged my mom to take me to the fire station instead of going home because I legitimately couldn't get air into my lungs. I was beginning to panic, and I didn't want to die on the way home. My mom reluctantly dropped me off and told me later to let her know when I was ready to be picked up from the hospital. She was so done with these issues and all the doctor bills that were piling up weekly.

The fire department answered the door and I quickly gasped what was going on. I told them I couldn't breathe (which was pretty obvious), and they put me in the back of their ambulance to check me out. I was quickly tiring and couldn't hardly say anything because of the situation. My heart rate was high, and my oxygen and carbon dioxide levels were off, so they decided to take me to the hospital with lights and sirens.

The guy in the back with me was administering medications to help combat the reaction and giving me high-flow oxygen to help my breathing. I still couldn't get air into my lungs. I was too far gone, and the meds weren't helping. I was deteriorating rapidly and started losing consciousness every now and then. The paramedic tried to keep me awake and said that if I fell asleep I would stop breathing, and he'd have to put a tube down my throat. That honestly didn't faze me. In fact, nothing did. Needles, IV's, poking, talking, it all just happened subconsciously without me really being aware. I didn't have enough energy to care or pay attention.

The sirens were blaring down the streets and freeways to the hospital. I was still trying to breathe but starting to give up. It was so hard and painful, and I was tired. The medic did his best to keep me awake and was talking to me while he gave me more emergency medicine. We finally made it to the hospital and I was taken into a room where a doctor and nurses were ready. They hooked me up to all the monitors and found things to be somewhat normal. Not too bad, even though I felt like crap. They gave me a nebulizer treatment, because it apparently wasn't a classic allergic reaction. My breathing regulated after a little while and left me exhausted.

I was surprised and frustrated with some of the people's responses to my body's obvious reactions. I couldn't breathe for the life of me and some people didn't even take it seriously. It had been happening a few times that week already, with some of the nurses acting as if I wasn't telling the truth, or just making it up. I knew I wasn't so the fact that they thought I was, bothered me. The problem was this kept happening every few days and I was blowing through my money because of Epi-Pen's, thinking that they were working a little bit. It wasn't until after three weeks of suffering; of going to the hospital over ten times, nine times by ambulance; of using about eighteen Epi-Pen's; and of draining most of the money in my bank account, that I was finally diagnosed with a very rare disorder called: Conversion Disorder.

To briefly explain what that is, it is basically a rare problem where my brain mimics the symptoms of major debilitating medical issues in response to normal every day stress...kind of as a way for my brain to cope with life. The doctor who diagnosed me with this said that I would have to live with this for the rest of my life, that there is no cure, treatment, or medication that can help, and that I need to limit stress as much as possible and just "deal with it." I couldn't believe it. What did that mean? I didn't fully understand the diagnoses for a long time until I started dealing with even more mysterious symptoms that wouldn't show up in testing.

Eight months later, after I had gotten out of the first mental hospital and went back to my friends home in West Texas, I had a hard time functioning. I was quickly fatigued and couldn't even walk in a straight line because I was so dizzy. I was dealing with vertigo, daily becoming nauseous and hardly able to move. I constantly had headaches that would occasionally turn into migraines. My bed and the couch were where I spent the majority of the day, and after a week of being there in that condition my dad came to pick me up and drive me the six hours back home to my family. I kept waiting for things to get better physically because I didn't know what in the world could be causing this. But it didn't. For a few weeks this went on, and I became more frustrated and depressed because I couldn't do anything.

It was becoming absolutely ridiculous. I finally looked up my symptoms and found that it was looking like I may have a brain tumor. I tried to not freak out, but because of the severity of the situation it was hard not to. I convinced my mom to take me to the doctor and they agreed that it seemed like something was going on in my brain. They ordered an MRI and I waited for the results. All I wanted were answers and some type of treatment. When I went in for the diagnoses, I found out that surprisingly everything came back normal. Here I was, with symptoms of a brain tumor, but no results to show it.

Because everything checked out fine, it was clear that this was yet again a result of the Conversion Disorder. It had been about a year since I was first diagnosed, and I was having to figure out how to distinguish true medical emergencies and side effects or symptoms of this disorder. It made sense, but it was a hard pill to swallow. To think that my body would react like that and mimic a brain tumor was disturbing. I now would have to just wait for the symptoms to go away. A week later I began feeling better, and within two and a half weeks was back to normal.

However, it wasn't long until I had another bout of stress related issues. Only about a month later, I woke up and tried to get out of bed, but I couldn't. My legs wouldn't move and felt like a dead weight to me. I literally fell out of bed and army crawled to the bathroom. Afterwards, I crawled out into the kitchen and pulled myself onto a chair, waiting for my mom to get up. She came out of her bedroom and when I explained my predicament, she didn't understand how I just suddenly couldn't move my legs.

For a little while she and a few other people thought I wasn't trying hard enough, or even maybe was making it up. But I wasn't making it up, I was trying, and I couldn't believe it either. I didn't understand how I was supposed to practice moving my legs when they were practically disconnected from me, not communicating with my brain, and refused to move. Every day I tried, and every day my legs wouldn't budge. I army crawled across the cement path to get to the car and army crawled all over the house on both rough carpet and tile. My knees and elbows quickly became bruised and scratched up. As time went on, I was slowly starting to accept the fact that I was essentially paralyzed from the waist down and that I may never walk again. I knew that this was the Conversion Disorder and that my brain was in a sense rebooting itself, but I was unsure of how exactly it worked and if I would ever regain the use of my legs.

After a little over a week of crawling and being in quite a bit of pain as a result, I finally found a cheap wheelchair that someone was selling online. My mom and I went and picked it up, finally giving my knees and elbows a chance to heal. My life was very different now. Not being able to drive or do things on my own, not being able to get from one room to the next without a ramp and having to rely solely on my family to reach the dishes or get things down for me. Getting dressed was tricky and took about five to ten minutes to do. Taking a shower was almost impossible sometimes, so we had to put a chair in there.

I didn't realize until that time how much I had taken advantage of the simple things in life. My mom had to force me out of the wheelchair, because I didn't know what to do; I thought that maybe I would regain movement as quickly as I had lost it, that it would just get better one day. But she had to make me move. I was in that chair for five weeks before my brain decided to let things work again. It took another week or two to go from wheelchair to walker, to walking on my own. Mind you, this had happened all because my body couldn't handle any kind of stress. At all. And it was something that I had no control over.

Having a disorder like this was extremely frustrating, and a huge cause for my depression. Nobody could understand what this was and quickly blamed me for my own medical issues. Because it was triggered by stress, and nothing ever showed up in medical testing, people would look at me with these annoyed faces and say that I was just doing it for attention. I didn't understand why they would believe that crap but struggled to understand the disorder myself. I had been dealing with random undiagnosed health issues for so long, that I most likely had this issue for a couple years prior to being diagnosed. Often, I would cry out of frustration and anger, as even some doctors didn't know what it was.

Thus, began my forever journey of a life with Conversion Disorder. A rare, and misunderstood problem.

CHAPTER 12

Seize

At the early age of four years old, I was diagnosed with epilepsy producing grand mal seizures. Vivid memories haunted me even after I stopped having them all together at the age of twelve. The epilepsy was a juvenile type that I could grow out of during my early teenage years. I did, and my brain waves normalized. However, the fear that was produced from that time never really left me. I kept pushing it to the back of my head, trying to move on and believe that I truly would never have to go through that hell again. It was way too terrifying.

In 2013, I graduated high school and went straight to a trade school close by. I went to study to become an Emergency Medical Technician (EMT) and work on the back of an ambulance. Trade school was awesome. It was hard at times, but I was learning about something I loved so it made it more fun. After attending for a month, I got my first job as a waitress at a small cafe. I had to learn how to balance work, school, and homework, and the environment I was working in wasn't the best. It was October at this point, and I had finished almost all of my homework for school. The next month would be clinicals, and then finals.

I went to my first twelve-hour shift at a local hospital and worked at night. I was trying to fill out one of my patient forms on the counter in the Emergency Room at about three o'clock a.m. Suddenly, my head dropped briefly, and I blacked out for a second. I looked around to see if anyone had noticed, but thankfully no one had. I continued my work trying to ignore what just happened, thinking maybe I was just too tired. The next morning when I came home, I told my mom and both of us looked at each other in temporary confusion. We dismissed it as just something that had to do with fatigue.

A week later, I was sitting at the dinner table talking with my family when it happened again. My head dropped, my eyes rolled back, and I briefly lost consciousness. My mom instantly was concerned since she had just witnessed the second one, and I was becoming a bit frightened that the seizures had come back, only in a different form.

It wasn't long before I had one at work while carrying dirty dishes. I dropped them as I blacked out and broke a plate and coffee mug. My face quickly turned red hot and my heart was racing. What had I done? I dropped a customer's food order a few days later and had to get that remade. It was getting to be a problem. I realized that I was most likely dealing with drop seizures, a form of epilepsy. So, I quit my job for that and other reasons and tried to figure out what my next steps would be. It wasn't long until I began randomly twitching. They were what seemed to be muscle spasms and it was occasionally interrupting whatever I was doing. The spasms only lasted a few months and then stopped just as suddenly as they had come.

October of 2014 took an unexpected turn. I started having episodes of violent jerking where one side of my body would seize up and jerk over to the other side. The episodes started out lasting twenty to thirty minutes, where I couldn't walk anywhere because I'd fall over with a jerk. I practically fell off the couch or bed that I was on and had to be careful not to hurt myself. During this violent time, I quickly became exhausted and unable to talk much. Once it had passed, I would be quite weak and tired.

As weeks went on of this happening numerous times, it began to strengthen. The episodes became longer and more frequent. It came to a point where it was occurring twice a day and lasting up to four hours at a time. I was seeing a neurologist and after scans and testing, I was diagnosed with myoclonic jerking and a non-epileptic form of seizures called Psychogenic Nonepileptic Seizures (PNES) which was rare. After a few months of jerking and losing sleep I was put on a muscle relaxant for the seizures, an anti-anxiety medication which almost completely stopped the episodes. I learned later that PNES is closely associated with the rare Conversion Disorder.

In January, I started having a different type of seizure and the medication stopped working. I would wake up with my jaw locked, fists clenched, and my back would suddenly arch up in a contraction. My eyes would roll back in my head and I couldn't breathe. The arching would last for about thirty seconds and then stop. My body would be weak and sore, as this happened up to eight times in a fifteen-minute span before letting up completely. My confusion and frustration grew as I experienced these once a week, not sure what exactly it was. The medication wasn't doing anything for me anymore, so we went back to the neurologist to see what he suggested. He said it was the PNES rearing its ugly head again, only in a different type of seizure. I was then put on an anti-seizure medication which helped immediately and was weaned off within two months.

Just when I thought this was over, something hit

yet again. Seven months after my last seizure I was dealing with constant allergic reactions at work (as described in the previous chapter). I kept working in spite of them and decided to go to a natural chiropractic doctor who did a type of therapy to treat all the functions in my body that were attacking itself. It had been suggested to me by a friend and since I was desperate, I tried it.

I went into the office on September 29th, 2015 for my first treatment. Not to long into it, I began to feel very strange. I was supposed to be relaxing but I couldn't. I began to sweat profusely, felt my chest tightening, and was very thirsty. I called out for someone to come help and the assistants came in trying to figure out what was going on, and what to do about it. One of them got a wet rag and wiped my forehead to try and cool me down. They brought me a paper cup of water to drink from, and I guzzled it down. My body was starting to make sudden twitching movements, but I had never felt like this before. This was totally different. I didn't know if this was a panic attack, or a reaction to the treatment, or what. I was quickly tiring and could hardly speak.

Suddenly out of nowhere, I started seizing up. I was laying on a skinny adjusting table having a full on grand mal seizure -- one that I'd never hoped to have again. I was vaguely aware of what was going on, but I couldn't communicate, talk, breathe, or think properly. My fear was coming true. It was happening. The staff called 911, and the fire department that I volunteered with at the time showed up and assessed the situation. The seizure had stopped by the time they got there, so they took my vitals and loaded me onto the stretcher. I was still quite out of it when it happened again. I started seizing while they were wheeling me out of the chiropractic office and into the ambulance. After about a minute or two it stopped and they all jumped in trying to do something to help, either by hooking me up to oxygen or the heart monitor, or starting an IV, or giving me medication. The last thing I vaguely remember, was the paramedic saying my blood sugar was low and my heart rate and oxygen were a little off. They raced me to the hospital as I was completely unaware of my surroundings.

The next thing I remember was not until a few hours later. I could hear my mom anxiously talking to people on the phone with a choked-up voice, explaining the condition I was in. I was still too much in an unconscious state to really understand what was going on, open my eyes, move, or even speak. Hearing was all I had, and that was every now and then. I could feel this cold stuff dripping down my arm and I felt sweaty everywhere. I heard my mom panic as she saw my arm and called for the nurse. Apparently, I had been seizing every few minutes for four hours, and none of the medications were working. I had pulled my IV during one of the seizures and that was blood that I felt dripping down my arm. Not too much longer and I began having another seizure, and I could vaguely hear my mom crying in the background. Nobody could do anything but watch me and make sure I didn't hurt myself.

This continued for many more hours of which I hardly remember anything. I was in and out of consciousness, only becoming briefly aware for a few minutes before falling into unconsciousness again for a few hours. It was finally arranged for me to be transported by ambulance to a larger hospital in Dallas, Texas, about an hour west from where I was at. We arrived there a little after midnight and my seizures were finally starting to be less frequent. I was hooked up to an EEG monitor to look at my brain wave patterns for the next few days. I had at that point been constantly seizing for sixteen hours and never fully woke up until late the next morning.

I opened my eyes for the first time in 24 hours and looked around the room. My dad was there, and I had wires hooked up to me all over the place. I started hallucinating because of all the medication in my system, which kind of concerned my dad. I was there for three days, having seizures a few times a day, unable to walk, and extremely weak. Once the testing surprisingly came back normal, they said it must have been the Psychogenic Nonepileptic Seizures and released me home. I had to use a walker for a few weeks since my legs didn't really work after all that and the seizures eventually became less and less.

That was honestly one of the hardest physical things I've had to experience and caused a lot of anxiety and emotional trauma. It was a huge eye opener to the nature of PNES, and the intense seizure symptoms it can produce because of normal stress in life. I was very glad when those seizures did stop and feared their return. It wasn't until almost two years later that I started having similar issues again. I knew the feeling, which was terrifying in and of itself.

I was at a friend's apartment cleaning when the feeling hit, and I explained to him what was going to happen and what he needed to do. I laid down on the floor surrounded by blankets, took off my jewelry, and my breathing became labored and increased while my body started feeling weird as it came. Once the seizure hit I seized up, jerking, contracting, and not really breathing for a period of time. The seizure passed, and I was breathing hard, my body in recovery mode, all contorted until the next seizure hit a few minutes later. This pattern continued for about an hour leaving me weak, sore, exhausted, and drenched in sweat. It took another half hour before I was able to speak and sit up. My hands were all cramped up and unable to straighten for a while, so my friend had to give me water himself.

I fully recovered, but this would become a weekly occurrence sometimes happening twice a week. The same feeling would come, the same thing would happen, and the aftermath was always the same. However, it did get to a point where I lost the ability to talk completely. I could not communicate with anyone for about a week because I was not able to form words. It was a symptom, I guess, of having had so many seizures and the connection between my brain and my voice became messed up. I began writing down whatever I wanted to say, and eventually downloaded an app on my phone to speak for me.

The strange thing about these seizures, though, was that I could hear what was going on, but I could not control what was happening to me, could not communicate, could not breathe (I was just occasionally gasping), and could not see. I was somewhat aware of my surroundings but trapped inside my own body and completely unable to control the situation. My friend did have to call an ambulance one night because I wasn't breathing enough in-between seizures. He got scared and called, though the episodes had ended by the time the fire department got there. These types of seizures too, eventually stopped.

Even now, I occasionally will have a staring seizure if I've had a stressful day or am exhausted. I stare off into the distance with my eyes crossed and pupils dilated from anywhere between twenty minutes to an hour. The left side of my body will twitch every now and then, and once I come out of it I can't talk for a little while, am extremely thirsty, my speech is slurred later, and my hands are cramped up for awhile while I recover. The process is quite exhausting.

These seizures haunt me because I have a rare condition that can make these symptoms resurface at any given time...all because of stress. Natural, everyday stress. And I have to constantly live with this fear -- or reality -- for the rest of my life. A life with PNES.

CHAPTER 13

Abuse

Conversion Disorder is a rare disorder and Psychogenic Nonepileptic Seizures are not commonly talked about because of how difficult it is to diagnose, and oftentimes has been a source for misdiagnosis. It can be very uncomfortable and challenging to both the doctor and the patient suffering from the seizures to properly diagnose and figure out treatment. Though there are many people dealing with PNES, it is mostly talked about behind closed doors because of the negative stigma associated with mental health in our society, as well as the frustration that comes along with having that diagnoses.

I personally don't know anyone else who has my condition, though I know there are people out there. It is quite hard to specifically diagnose Conversion Disorder due to the odd mimicking symptoms, and doctors not being aware or knowing about this disorder. I was symptomatic and misdiagnosed for over five years before finally being properly diagnosed, and definitely wished I knew sooner.

The struggle with Conversion Disorder is that the symptoms you experience can be triggered by an actual illness or injury and get extraordinarily worse, excessively drawing out the recovery process. It can also come on suddenly without warning with severe symptoms that are usually debilitating. The person dealing with these things also doesn't know if there is something medically going on or if it's just the disorder, which then procures a substantial amount of doctor visits, testing, and medical bills.

When Conversion Disorder rears its ugly head, it is triggered by stress, some conscious, and some subconscious. It is sometimes quite a bit, but at times it only takes a small amount of stress to cause your brain and body to react. Most of it is daily stress that is out of your control. Other times the stress is from just learning what your limits are and sometimes overstepping those boundaries. When trying to describe my disorder to someone, I always have to explain how hard it is to just "not be stressed" because they usually tell me that if I would stop being stressed I wouldn't have any problems. So, to answer them in my words I always say: life equals stress. Life is full of it! You can't escape anxiety or stress without becoming a hermit and never coming out of your room. And if you were to do that depression would most likely set in. When you put all these pieces together, there seems to be no escaping this problem.

Another thing that happens with Conversion Disorder, though, is that the stress can sometimes build up over time. For me, it can be about every six to ten months that something major and debilitating happens to me, as a result of collective, every day natural stress. I may one day just randomly wake up with a problem or I might have a minor injury that will suddenly "get worse" and more painful. The mind kind of has a mind of its own.

Imagine a cup, very slowly filling with water, until it reaches the top, then it overflows, sometimes knocking over the cup of water. That is like a person dealing with Conversion Disorder. They have everyday stress that comes into their lives and builds up over time. They may not think they have a problem because they are handling it well and doing the right things to cope with their stress or anxiety, when on the inside, their mind and body are freaking out. It's as if the brain doesn't register that anything is being done to cope with the stress. Once the stress level reaches a breaking point, all hell breaks loose, and it overflows into a debilitating medical issue in order to cope. It is literally the only way their body can handle what life gives them. It is a way to reboot or give the brain a chance to take a break and restart.

Once the dam breaks, it actually starts immediately relieving stress and anxiety as the debilitating medical issue is the body's way of recovering and rejuvenating itself. It is the feeling you get after throwing up. You feel so much better after getting all of it out, even though it's still exhausting. It releases all that pent-up energy, adrenaline, stress, and anxiety, making it easier to breathe once it's all over.

One of the major side effects of dealing with Conversion Disorder and PNES is that it can cause severe depression, anxiety, and sometimes even suicidal tendencies. Due to the sudden, sporadic, and severe medical issues that show up sometimes with no warning, it is easy to become depressed or anxious. You do not know what the next day will hold or what might happen. You could be bed ridden from a sudden medical issue or not be able to drive, which means that you would have little to no interaction with the outside world and an unknown time frame of how long this will last. It can cause suicidal thoughts because it is so hard to be successful in the world with this condition and it can make you feel extremely worthless, handicapped, useless, and sometimes even stupid.

In my life of living with this disorder, I have had symptoms of Multiple Sclerosis, a brain tumor, a torn muscle that was almost surgically operated on until the MRI results came back, grand mal seizures, anaphylactic shock (severe allergic reactions), temporary paralysis, chronic dizziness, blood pressure issues, and Hypothyroidism. I had all these symptoms, but no test results to show any cause for it. When you have a chronic debilitating medical problem and you don't know if it's serious or not, it costs a fortune to have to constantly be going to the doctor to get tests done, only to hear that "nothing is wrong with you."

Another huge problem regarding Conversion Disorder and PNES is that hardly *anybody* knows how to respond appropriately to the situation. Because it's not commonly talked about and yet still considered a mental disorder, most people think it's "in their heads," or that the person is just "making it up" for attention. It can be an open door for abuse, physically, emotionally, and mentally, easily producing trauma and allowing for misunderstanding and conflict. It can also be a door for people to treat you without respect, compassion, or in an inappropriate way. I personally have experienced both emotional and mental kinds of abuse, as well as completely inappropriate actions of a mental health worker violating my physical boundaries, similar (but not quite) to physical abuse. I have mainly experienced them because of my stress-induced seizures, due to my being incapacitated. Here are two specific stories:

The first instance was while I was in a mental rehab facility in Washington. I started having a seizure in a chair in one of the quiet rooms, and one of the other patients saw me and got the staff. I had listed seizures on my medical history form, but because of protocol, they had to call an ambulance. By the time the fire department crew got to the facility, the seizure had stopped but I still was not fully awake yet. I could hear things going on, though some of it was fuzzy and I could not communicate or open my eyes. I mean seriously, it's exhausting to have a seizure even when brought on by stress and anxiety. The medics came over and tried to wake me, to which I couldn't respond. They checked my vitals, which were all good, and decided that I must be faking it. They broke open the smelling salts which almost stopped my breathing because of the intensity of the smell. It didn't "wake me" like they wanted it to, because my body seems to have its own time schedule. So, they broke another smelling salt which had the same effect; I couldn't breathe, I still couldn't wake up, and they were all saying I was just faking it for attention.

A few of them started to pack up and talk in the hall or load the rig. After a little while, I regained full consciousness, though I couldn't talk right away. There was one paramedic who was getting ready to walk out of the room to whom I tried to explain what happened on a pad of paper. I was writing frantically, trying to get him to understand that I wasn't faking it and that I have this disorder. I wanted him to understand what had happened and let him know that smelling salts don't work, that it actually makes things worse. I was frustrated with how they had handled the situation by belittling me and this disorder that I had no control over. However, he just kept saying that he understands I think it's something else, but to not "do that again", and if I need someone to talk to, well, I was at a mental rehab facility, so I was at the right place. I could tell he didn't believe a word I was writing and that I was wasting his time. He walked out, and I was left with tears coming down my face, frustrated, and still panting for air from those darn smelling salts that had practically made me stop breathing.

The second instance was while I was in the second mental health hospital. I had tried to commit suicide, and then once caught, I was put in a separate room with no covers and a guard watching my every move. During the afternoon of the next day I felt a seizure coming on. I told the guard who got one of the staff, and I laid down on that bare mattress on the floor. My diagnosis of PNES was on my health history chart, so they were supposed to know about them. I began seizing and because I could still hear what was going on around me, I heard the staff person tell me to knock it off. I could not respond at this point since I was actively seizing and barely breathing, so she threatened me. She said she'd take off my clothes if I didn't stop. I literally couldn't. So, she did. She somehow managed to take my clothes off while I was seizing and then began threatening me further since I "still wouldn't stop."

This lady kept telling me to knock it off, told me I was faking this, and she wasn't going to buy into it. She then threatened to take off my bra and underwear next if I continued. I was having a seizure triggered by stress, and this was not helping at all, especially since I didn't have any control of what was happening. My seizing continued as it normally did because I was out of control in this situation and I couldn't stop it even though I wanted to. As a result, this ridiculous mental hospital worker took off my undergarments, leaving me lying there seizing completely naked. And I'm not joking...she left. Walked out of the room with all my clothing because she was so ticked off and I guess waiting for me to "shape up."

After a little while longer, I finally stopped, and she eventually came back a little bit later with some paper hospital scrubs, refusing to give me back any of my clothes. I was livid. She wouldn't listen to anything I had to say once I had recovered from the seizure and ignored me. I never saw her again, but I checked out of the facility the next day against medical advice because of the inappropriate actions of the staff at this mental hospital. I had been violated. Exposed and completely embarrassed. My debilitation had been taken advantage of.

This was not okay.

CHAPTER 14

Acceptance

As you can see from these examples in the previous chapter, it is very easy to be abused due to the vulnerable state the person is in that is out of their hands. Also because of a lack of information to the public, and even to healthcare workers about these disorders. They are *real* issues. The brain reacts differently in people with Conversion Disorder and PNES, and the way it releases stress is through these debilitating and sometimes harmful situations. While having seizures, I oftentimes hurt myself because I would run into walls, bed frames, or couches. My wrists and hands would be bruised because they would pound together during the seizing process. Some people have fallen off ladders and down stairs. And to reinstate, these are completely out of the control of the sufferer.

These people do not *want* to have a seizure, so why would you think that someone is faking it and then abuse them in return? No, this is a misconnection in the brain that is triggered by normal life stresses. Not abnormal brain discharges as most people with epilepsy would have, but rather just different communication between the brain and the body in response to certain situations.[13] The person suffering from these seizures may develop more trauma because of the sudden, painful, terrifying process of having a seizure. And the frustration that comes from not knowing, not getting diagnosed or misdiagnosed, and not being able to get treatment, is awful.

So, for all the doctors, nurses, medical personnel, and the general public, please consider these things when encountering someone with either one of these disorders.

Your Words: As you may have remembered in previous chapters, the number one thing *not* to say, is that they are faking it, have made it up, brought this on themselves, or that it's their fault. All those phrases have been said to me numerous times, and it is NOT helpful in any way. It is very harmful. It hurts to have someone blame your pain and suffering on yourself. It can hinder their trust towards you and will elevate the stress levels that they already have which is the opposite of what needs to happen. Instead of saying those things, say that

---

[13] "FAQ's about psychogenic nonepileptic seizures." *PNES Psychogenic Nonepileptic Seizures*, 2011-2018, nonepilepticseizures.com/epilepsy-psychogenic-NES-faqs-what-are.php. Accessed 23 Aug 2018

you're there for them and that they can get through this. Most people dealing with these disorders are actually victims of trauma, whether little or big, from their childhood or more recently, so keep that in mind when you encounter someone.[14] Your words mean a lot to those you talk to and can be a negative or positive influence. Watch what you say. Be validating and understand that these disorders are not an easy thing for anyone to deal with.

Listen: Ways that people can eliminate some of their stress is by talking about what is going on in their lives, thus not allowing the anxieties to build up internally. As a result, you should be a listener. Talking through their feelings and emotions can be very therapeutic for them. They need you to listen and help them through it by just being there.

Annoyance: A good number of people that I have encountered -- including some of my own family members -- are easily annoyed by any medical issues I have. They might roll their eyes and sigh when they see me in a wheelchair, or having a seizure, or just having

---

[14] Norman, Abby "It's Not All In Your Head: Unraveling The Mystery Of Conversion Disorder." *ati*, 2015, allthatsinteresting.com/conversion-disorder. Accessed 23 Aug 2018

another medical issue. They act like I'm a burden, or just one big problem. It hurts. It causes stress and my anxiety levels to go up, also producing a lack of trust as well. Please don't show annoyance. They need you to accept them for who they are and to be there for them when they are suffering. As I've mentioned numerous times in each section, it's not their fault or under their control, so don't make them feel like it is.

Include: Just because someone is suffering physically doesn't mean they can't still enjoy things. So, invite them to do fun activities with you or a group of people. It can actually speed up the healing process when you help to temporarily relieve that anxiety, letting them have fun and laugh. Enjoyment is a very positive thing during that time. Living with these disorders is very depressing especially since there really isn't much hope for a cure at this point in time. Making sure to include them in your outings will make them feel special and give them a bit of normalcy to their life.

Help: If you know someone struggling with one of these disorders, see how you can help. If they are dealing with seizures, make sure you can create a safe place for them if they have a seizure while you're around and don't leave them in a room by themselves. Make sure there is nothing they can hurt themselves on, and if there is, put padding there. If they can't walk, help push them around. If they feel like they need to go to the hospital offer to take them yourself. Lend a helping hand whenever you can and do it out of compassion and joy, not irritation or disgust.

Friend: Most of all, be their friend. Friends quickly walk out of relationships because of limitations, disabilities and other issues, but don't be that person. Be the one that stays no matter what. One that is encouraging and helpful. One that listens more than they talk. One that never gets bothered and annoyed at any frequency of the disorder's attacks. Everyone needs a friend. So be that.

For all the people reading this who either have Conversion Disorder or PNES -- or both -- I want you to know that you are not in this alone. Yes, it is rare, and yes, it does suck, but there are ways to lessen the amount or frequency of these issues. Currently, it is still unknown exactly what causes Conversion Disorder and if it can be cured by any one thing, though it can be improved over time in some people. Even though Psychogenic Nonepileptic Seizures isn't a very common diagnosis, up to thirty-three people out of one-hundred thousand have the disorder[15] meaning that you are not the only one. The general public as well as some medical personnel don't know how to respond to these different problems

---

[15] "The Truth about Psychogenic Nonepileptic Seizures." *Epilepsy Foundation*, 2007, epilepsy.com/article/2014/3/truth-about-psychogenic-nonepileptic-seizures. Accessed 23 Aug 2018

that we struggle with, and some have never even heard of it before. I think that now is our chance to speak up and bring these painful and uncomfortable disorders to the light.

To help those dealing with Conversion Disorder, here are a few things that I have learned.

Belief: Although there are many people that tell you these medical conditions are your fault, and that you "obviously" have control over them, don't buy into that lie. None of this is your fault, and you can't change the way your brain is responding to these different situations.[16] A huge step in being able to stay positive and potentially cut down the frequency of episodes, is to believe the truth, and accept it for what it is. You have this disorder, and this is part of your story -- of who you are. And that's okay. This is something that can make you much stronger of a person. You just have to know that none of this is on you because that is way too big of a burden to carry anyways. Tune out the lies because those will bring you down. People can respond how they want and that's on them, not on you. But believe the

---

[16] "GARD Genetic and Rare Diseases Information Center." *Conversion Disorder*, 2017, rarediseases.info.nih.gov/diseases/6191/conversion-disorder. Accessed 23 Aug 2018

truth about the disorders. As hard as it is, try your very best to tune out the lies and the comments that bring you down.

Stress: Life is a big world full of stress. And sometimes we can't avoid it. With Conversion Disorder, I like to say that I'm essentially allergic to life. I know that stress is not always the reason behind this disorder, but it is for me and for others like me out there. In all reality though, for those whose body has stress trigger the physical problems, your body can't seem to handle any amount of stress that life throws at it. It basically wants you to become a hermit, living in your room all the time just sleeping and eating. However, that would produce depression, lethargy, and possibly suicidal tendencies. So how do you live life in balance? Well, it's a learning process. I'm still learning, but I've seen that listening to my body when it needs a break is a good thing. I still have fun, live a mostly normal young adult life with good friends that I trust, have low key jobs, and just try to make sure I don't overdo it. It can be unavoidable at times, with certain situations that you run into that are out of your control. But if you know that you did everything possible in your hands to avoid or eliminate stress, then when something physically happens you know you did your part and now it's your body's turn to get rid of the remaining stress.

Communicate: Part of helping to relieve stress, is by talking and communicating with people about your feelings and emotions. You can't keep them all to yourself. Talk to friends or family. Talk to a counselor regularly. Make sure you allow yourself to feel, but don't bottle it up inside. Just talking about what's been going on in your life can help release that built up stress.

Color: This may sound strange, but coloring and drawing can be relaxing. Periods of relaxation are key to cutting down the frequency of physical issues. Set times to rest by reading a book, coloring, or drawing. Making sure you have time for you will help bring the anxiety of the day down.

Positivity: When dealing with a medical issue, it's usually debilitating and frustrating. Staying positive can be extremely hard, but if you are able to be positive throughout that time it may help the recovery be faster. Remember that this medical issue is temporary...it will not last forever. Remind yourself that your brain is kind of rebooting itself, which is not a bad thing, though usually inconvenient. Try and stay positive, knowing that this will get better, and that this is your body's way of recharging. Don't fight it.

For those of you dealing with PNES, here are a few helpful tips for you.

Inform: One thing that has helped me when I have seizures is to inform the people I hang out with the most. I explain the disorder, what to expect, what it looks like, and what to do or not to do. I have always had a warning sign before they came, so it gave me a chance to get in a spacious room and tell a friend what was going on. The things I tell them is to make sure I don't hurt myself and try and put blankets or pillows in different places to ensure that I don't. I also tell them that I will be fine after a couple seizures, so don't call 911 unless I stop breathing for five minutes and turn blue. I make sure they understand that it will be scary, that it's not easy, and is very hard to watch, but that there are only a few things that help. They could panic if you don't say anything which would not help the situation at all. Another thing you can do is print out an explanation of what you have and what to do if anyone should encounter seeing you having one. I have put those in my wallet and in my car. The more people you inform, the less likelihood you have of added unnecessary stress while seizing.

Therapy: There are some types of intensive therapies called Eye Movement Desensitization Reprocessing (EMDR)[17] that are working to drastically decrease the amount of seizures individuals have daily,

---

[17] "What is EMDR?" *EMDR Institute, Inc.*, 2018, emdr.com/what-is-emdr/. Accessed 23 Aug 2018

weekly, or monthly. It involves figuring out and facing the fears, trauma, and stress of the past, dealing with them head on, all while being in a safe environment. I have not yet tried it, but it might be something you'd want to investigate.

Stress: Eliminating what stress you can (because you can't eliminate all), can help to decrease the seizures, or lessen the intensity or length. Talking about how you feel -- all your emotions and thoughts -- help more than you might think. Talk to friends and family you trust. Talk to a licensed counselor. Don't let your emotions and feelings stay pent up inside, because that alone could cause a seizure. A few other things that help are eating better, exercising regularly, coloring, resting, doing your favorite hobby, and just having fun. Laughter is always helpful in most all situations. Resting is also very important as well, so make sure you get enough sleep. The combination of lack of sleep and the normal stress of life, can trigger a seizure. So, make sure to get enough sleep as much as you can. These things help to manage your stress and help build up your self-esteem, which can be low due to the seizures.

Friends: Make sure you have people to help walk you through this. You can't do this by yourself. Find support groups if you have to on social media. Have at least a few friends that will have your back and make any seizures go smoother. Being scared and terrified while going through the seizing process is normal -- I usually always feel that way. But having a friend by your side helps to ease some of that anxiety. So, find some good, trustworthy friends.

To conclude this chapter, I want to emphasize the fact that both Conversion Disorder and PNES are real issues that are beyond our control. It may look fake, but it's not. It is our body's way of getting rid of a foreign invasion -- an unwanted intruder called stress. In some people though, they still don't know what the triggers are, if any. We do our best to eliminate our stress, but we can't avoid it all. These disorders probably make us stronger than most, always challenging our ability to keep going. We've constantly gone through hell and high water and every time have pulled through with more fight and strength than before. So, don't look down on people with these disorders. Instead, stand by them, encourage them, be a friend, and show them how valued they are!

Conclusion

I want to thank you for reading this book. I know it was not easy and possibly disturbing at times, but this was something I felt I needed to write. Depression, anxiety, PTSD, and self-harm are all very prominent issues around the world. There is also not a whole lot of understanding about these issues, what it's like, and how to respond. Conversion Disorder and Psychogenic Nonepileptic Seizures are rare conditions that still need to be known. This book was written in hopes of encouraging someone, giving light to a person in confusion, or possibly even saving a life.

I hope that this was very helpful for you, whether you're dealing with these issues yourself or know someone who is. This is very near to my heart and I take these things extremely seriously. I have felt that God wanted to use my story to impact somebody's life, no matter their religion, because it honestly doesn't matter. I just know that each person has a story and each story is unique, and every story can be used for good...if only it is told. This is my story of victory. Because victory comes in surviving. In learning and growing through the struggle. Victory is being able to come out on the other side stronger, and especially alive. So now my story has been told. My story from Struggle to Victory.

A Special Thanks

...to God who inspired me to write this book and gave me insight.

...to my family who supported me through this process, and have learned many things, growing in their knowledge of these mental issues.

...to all the lovely ladies at Carter BloodCare in Plano, TX, who encouraged me to keep writing and listened to my story: specifically, April, Nicole, Brenda, and Alexa.

...to my friends who helped me through the times that I was suicidal. Thank you, Jesse, Connor, Peggy, Athena, JD and Chrissy! Thank you for helping to keep me alive.

...to Thomas, who was a huge help during all of the issues I went through. Thank you for pointing me to Jesus, being a listener, being open, and speaking truth into my life!

...to my church family at Believers Chapel, Dallas, who stood by me when my Conversion Disorder debilitated me, and depression encompassed me. Thank you for being such an encouragement, for praying for me, and for standing with me through each trial and victory.

...to my 2017-2018 Core Bible study group, who helped me and encouraged me through the trials and through the writing of this book. You all are incredible young ladies!

...to Madi, Emma, and Charis, who helped this book get published by helping with the necessary editing. I couldn't have done this without you!

...and especially to my counselor, who has listened, given me great advice, not judged, and given me hope when I felt hopeless. Thank you, Eddie!

Made in the USA
Columbia, SC
24 April 2023

15716162R00085